Better Than Good

ADOLPH W. NEWTON
with WINSTON ELDRIDGE

BETTER *than* GOOD

A BLACK SAILOR'S WAR
1943–1945

Naval Institute Press • *Annapolis, Maryland*

Library of Congress Cataloging-in-Publication Data
Newton, Adolph W., 1925–
    Better than good : a Black sailor's war, 1943–1945 / Adolph W.
  Newton, with Winston Eldridge.
        p .   cm .
    ISBN 1-55750-649-3 (alk. paper)
     1. Newton, Adolph W., 1925– . 2. World War, 1939–1945—Naval
operations, American. 3. World War, 1939–1945—Personal narratives,
American. 4. United States. Navy—Afro-Americans—Biography.
5. Afro-American sailors—Biography. I. Eldridge, Winston, 1952– . II. Title.
D773.N495 1999
940.54'5973'092—dc21   98-38939

Contents

Acknowledgments

The publication of this book would not have been possible without a lot of help from a lot of people. While it would be impossible to list them all here, we would like to extend our sincere appreciation to Annabelle Hawkins, Thomas Mason, Carolyn Gaither-Ellis, Julia Woodward, Daisy Franklin, and Eugenia Collier. Thanks also to the staff of the Naval Reserve Officer Training Corps Museum at Hampton University, as well as the staff of the archives at the Hampton University Library. Endless appreciation to our families, who tolerated us through the process of completing the manuscript.

1 *Decision*

"Newton, Adolph Newton, letter for Newton," the mailman was calling.

My heart almost stopped beating as I moved to the door of the dayroom. "Over here, man, I'm Newton," I told him as I took the envelope and tried to calm down. "Thanks."

The mailman was teasing the rest of the guys as I moved away from the group crowded around the door. "That's it, gentlemen. Newton's the only one that got lucky today. Better luck next time." I eased into my seat, thinking a mile a minute. *Luck—you call this luck? No need to be scared now,* I told myself. *You done what you done, so you might as well face it.*

Although my friend Eddie was the only person who knew where I was, and even he wasn't sure exactly where, I just knew that the letter was from my mother, even before I looked at the return address. My mind was racing. *Can't open this right now. Suppose she's gonna make me come home? Just when I was*

starting to get comfortable. . . . How'd she find me so fast? Eddie musta told. . . .
Damn, motherfu—

I caught myself before I said it. Up until eight days ago, I had never even heard that word, and now I was using it almost as a reflex.

I walked around in a daze for the rest of the day, as if I had been drinking some of that cheap wine they sold at the corner store at home. *Maybe this is all a bad dream, and I'm about to wake up, maybe that's what's happening,* I told myself as I pulled the envelope out one more time. The envelope had been in and out of my pocket twenty times since lunch, and it was just past dinnertime. I shook the envelope to get everything on the side away from the stamp, took a deep breath, ripped the damned thing open, and started reading before I had a chance to change my mind.

> *My Dear Son,*
>
> *I want you to know, first of all, that your father and I knew where you were the day after you left. We are mad at you for running away to the war. You father said you have plenty of time for that after you turn eighteen. Why did you do this?*
>
> *I talked to the people at the recruitment office. It was our intention to bring you home, but they said that since you were going to be eighteen in six months, it would be better to let you stay, because you would enlist on your own as soon as you were old enough. If this is what you want to do, and this will make you happy, you may stay. Because of this your father and I will let you stay. I want you to write often, and may God bless you and guide you through your coming days.*
>
> *Love,*
> *Mother*

I breathed for the first time since I opened the envelope. I read the letter again and again to make sure I got it right. *I can stay!!!* I was so happy that I wrote an answer right away, as if my mother had put a time limit on the offer. I wrote it fast, even though I couldn't really get my thoughts together.

> *Dear Mother,*
>
> *I was very glad to hear from you. Thank you for letting me stay. I'm sorry I had to do it the way I did, but you know that you and Daddy would not have signed the papers for me. I'll write often. Thanks again.*
>
> *Your son,*
> *Adolph*

Now that everything was settled, I didn't know what to do. I was just glad that things had turned out the way I wanted. In my heart I knew that I had done the right thing. Taps didn't sound so sad that night.

This is a true story. It is about a young Negro who enlisted in the U.S. Navy during World War II. It is also about the ordinary people he met along the way—about their reactions to him and the beliefs they expressed concerning one of the greatest challenges ever to confront the American people: integration, or civil rights, as it is more commonly known. Integration may be right in the view of some people and wrong in the view of others, but it is a challenge that touches the lives of everyone, young or old.

In 1942, President Franklin D. Roosevelt issued a proclamation to all U.S. Navy commanders that the Navy was to be integrated, with the enlistment of Negroes in the Navy's Seaman-Fireman Branch first. There were no demonstrations for or against this historic proclamation, although feelings must have run high in both directions. The general public was so engrossed in the realization that we were at war that the order handed down by President Roosevelt to the Navy went out with little publicity. This might have been a big factor in the success of this endeavor.

As I listened to taps, my mind drifted back to that day two weeks before, in Baltimore, when I opened the door to the main post office and followed the signs to the Navy recruiting station. There was a white man in uniform reading a newspaper at the desk in front of the door. I walked up to him.

"Could you tell me who to talk to about joining?"

He lowered his paper and slowly looked me up and down before pointing his thumb toward a desk in the rear of the office. "See the chief." He returned to the paper.

"How do I know which one's the chief?" My confusion overpowered my nervousness.

"Straight to the back. You can't miss him," he answered without looking up.

I realized what he meant when I got to the last desk, where there was a coal-black man in a blue uniform with a lot of medals on the chest. This had to be the chief. He looked up and then stood and offered his hand.

"Can I help you?"

"I want to find out how to join the Navy."

"That's fine, son. What's your name?"

"Adolph Newton, sir."

"I'm not an officer; I'm Chief Petty Officer Jones, but you can just call me Chief. That's the way we do it in the Navy. Have a seat, Adolph." He pointed to a chair beside me. I sat, and he returned to his chair.

"Now, before we talk about anything else, how old are you, Adolph?"

I hesitated a moment before telling the truth: "Seventeen." I already knew what his response was going to be, and it wasn't what I wanted to hear.

"Well, Adolph, you have to be eighteen to enlist in the Navy on your own. You can join with your parents' consent. Will they sign the papers?"

"Yes," I lied. There was no way that my parents would sign that form. My three brothers were already in the Army, and there was no way my mother and father were going to let their baby go to war, too.

"Good. Now, you have two choices. There are two branches that we colored men can serve in, the Mess Attendant Branch and the Seaman-Fireman Branch."

"What's the difference?"

"The Mess Attendant Branch is responsible for serving meals to officers and cleaning their quarters. For a long time this was the only branch we could serve in, but President Roosevelt recently signed an executive order that said the Navy had to integrate. What that means to you is that you can try the Seaman-Fireman Branch if you want. That branch deals with the operation of the ship and firing the guns."

"That's what I'd like to try, the Seaman-Fireman part."

"No problem." He reached into a drawer, pulled out a folder, and took out some papers. He marked a couple of places on one of the forms. "I need you to take these home to your parents. They sign in the places marked with an X." He passed me the papers, which I folded the long way and put in my inside coat pocket. "Once you bring these back, we can take care of everything else. Any questions?"

"No, sir, I mean, no, Chief," I stuttered.

He laughed, rising from his chair. "Good, you learn fast." He shook my hand again and walked me to the door. "Your parents can give me a call if they have any questions. I'll see you soon."

I was busy thinking as I walked down the hall. I knew that the only way to get those papers signed was to do it myself. I buttoned my coat, getting ready for the January weather. As I walked out of the building, I heard a familiar voice.

"Adolph, what are you doing down here?" my sister Helen asked.

Man, I had to think fast. I patted my pocket to make sure the papers were still there. I was glad the coat had that inside pocket, because if she saw the papers, she'd know what I was doing.

"I had to come mail a package for Miss . . . Ethel," I answered, deliberately picking a lady who wasn't likely to run into anybody in my family. "She said it was real important, so I brought it down here so it would go out faster." *If you got to lie, might as well dress it up a little,* I thought.

"Well, I'll see you later," she said, preoccupied with her own plans. She went into the building.

I was a mess for the next couple of days. Evidently Helen didn't mention seeing me downtown, because my mother never said anything to me about it. I was glad of that, but I still had to find a way to get the papers signed. To me it was as simple as one-two-three, but when I added up the score, I always came up with . . . *me.* No matter how I figured it, I knew there was no way anybody but me was ever going to sign those papers. I had no choice, so I signed my parents' names.

I took the papers back to Chief Jones. He had some more forms for me to fill out. I signed my name so many times that my fingers got numb, but I was getting closer to being in the Navy, so I didn't mind. Finally the chief took me to an examination room.

"OK, strip, then go through the door to your right. That's where you'll get your physical. I'll see you when you're done."

I undressed quickly and went through the door. There were about twenty other men lined up, waiting to be examined by some Navy corpsmen, who were all white. My first impression as I looked down the line was that all men are *not* created equal. There were only a few other Negroes in this line. When I got to the first corpsman, I started to get a feeling for how slaves felt on the block.

"Where're your marks?" he asked.

"My what?" I asked, not sure that I had heard him.

"Your cut marks, knife cuts, razor cuts, like that."

"I don't have any," I answered, starting to get pissed off.

"You have to have some somewhere. Come on, now," he insisted.

"Look, I *don't* have any cut marks," I replied.

"All you colored boys got cut marks." He turned to another corpsman: "Hey, Joe, you ever seen a colored fella without cut marks?" he asked.

"Naw, every one I've ever seen has some, somewhere," the second corpsman answered.

"Well, this is one Negro that doesn't have any cut marks, and I'm not going to say it again."

By now I didn't care who knew I was upset. They had sense enough to drop the subject. The rest of the examination went smoothly, and soon I was back in with the chief. Of course he had some more papers for me to sign. I slid them back across the desk after I had finished.

"Adolph, everything's all taken care of. When do you want to leave?"

"I'll be ready in a week. Is that OK?"

"Sure. Be back here at 8 A.M. on January 28. You'll be sworn in, and then you'll leave for the naval training station at Great Lakes, Illinois. Welcome aboard." He got up and shook my hand.

I left the office happy, one step closer to being a sailor, but still needing to figure out a way to leave without my parents knowing what I was doing.

Things at home weren't easy, and they were getting worse. Every time I turned around I was getting into an argument with my father. He saw things his way, and I saw them my way. For a long time I'd been wanting to find a way to get out of the house. I wanted to join the Army, but that was out of the question as far as my parents were concerned, because my brothers were all in the Army. But as far as I was concerned, the Army would have been perfect. Whenever one of my brothers came home on leave, I would wear his uniform. I really liked the way I looked in it, and I liked the way it looked on me. I probably wouldn't have gone down to the recruiting station when I did, except that one day I got accused of breaking a dish, and my father kept saying something to me about it. After I had heard all I needed to hear, I left the house. The next thing I knew, I was at the post office. My father wasn't a bad man; I just had to get away from him; I had to get out of his house.

Even though I was only seventeen, I had been working ever since I could remember. I was born on 26 July 1925, in Baltimore, Maryland. My parents were Oscar Newton, who was from Warsaw, Virginia, and Helen Newton, who was born in Mount Winans, Maryland, a place in Baltimore that we Baltimoreans know as Westport. I was the youngest of six children, two girls and four boys. My sister Catherine was grown and living in New York by the time I was old enough to remember things. Helen, my other sister, is two years older than I. Ellsworth is fourteen years older, Vernon eight years, and Lloyd four years.

I was raised on Westwood Avenue. My childhood was what I would call normal. After school we would play basketball, football, or baseball, depending on the time of year. We would go sledding in the alley out back in the winter. Once I got a brand-new Western Flyer sled, and the first time I tried it out I slid into a shed and broke a couple of teeth. In the summer I would go out to my uncle's place in the country. I hated the country; I was always a city boy.

My father worked as a chef. He was always cooking something strange. The two things he cooked that I would never touch were turtle soup and muskrat. He was good with his hands, too. He had a little shop down in the cellar. He made a sailboat that I would float around in a little pond at the park. He kept a strap under the bed, and he knew how to use it.

My mother caught me smoking when I was about fourteen. She told me that if I was going to smoke, I might as well stop sneaking around doing it. After that day, I always smoked in the house. All of my brothers and sisters smoked, but women didn't smoke in public in those days.

My mother went to church regularly. We had to walk all the way downtown to church, and the service would last all day long—all of that on an empty stomach, because we usually wouldn't have breakfast before we left. My father didn't go to church, but he read the Bible before Sunday dinner. He wouldn't allow preachers in the house. The only preacher I can remember being in the house while my father was alive was Reverend Tapscott, who was my mother's cousin.

On one hand, I guess some people would think I had it made. When my brothers went into the service, I got all their clothes. I had all the suits and shoes I could want. There were always a few dollars in my pocket; I was working at a record shop, so I kept up with all the latest music. Clothes and music were always important to me. An example of this was Billy Eckstine; white people had Bing Crosby and Frank Sinatra, but we had Billy Eckstine and Arthur Prysock. The first time I saw him was at the Royal Theater in Baltimore with Earl Hines and his orchestra. Billy Eckstine had joined Earl Hines after winning the Amateur Hour at the Apollo Theater in Harlem. When Eckstine walked out on stage, the place got quiet. He had on a drape suit, which was the latest style, but his shirt and tie really attracted attention. The shirt had a spread collar, which we had never seen before. The collar had a six-inch spread with collar stays, and his tie was tied in a different way. It was a new knot called the "Duke of Windsor" knot. After this show, every store in Baltimore was selling spread-collar shirts as fast as they could get them, and everybody was trying to learn how to tie this knot. Billy Eckstine really made an impression on me, and on my friends, and on everyone else.

There were a lot of boys and girls my age in the neighborhood; we had all pretty much grown up together. My buddies were Al Coates, George Davis, Nathaniel Sharpes, Eddie Stanley, and Leonard Butler. We hung together, and there was a group of girls that were our age, so we were always around each other. There wasn't a whole lot of "going together," but we never had to worry about having somebody to dance with. We got a lot of practice on the popular dances—the Two-Step, the Georgia Grind, the Fish, the Jitterbug, we did them all. We had a lot of fun.

Even though there were lots of good times, I wasn't happy. I couldn't name any one particular thing that was wrong, but something wasn't right. I didn't care much about school at all. I would hook school whenever I got a chance because I just wasn't interested. When I was small, I enjoyed it. Every morning I would scrub the front steps before going to school; just about everybody in Baltimore had marble steps, but ours seemed to get dirtier than anybody else's. The elementary school, PS 112, was only about four blocks from our house; I could walk to school, and I came home for lunch. Mrs. Taylor, my art teacher, was one of my favorite teachers, along with Mrs. Lawrence. There was one teacher, Mrs. Rawlings, who was just pure evil. She had one of those eighteen-inch rulers, and it seemed like she lived to use that thing. I was in a writing contest once sponsored by the Afro-American newspaper. I won a prize—not first prize, but whatever prize it was, it was tickets to a show at the Regent Theater.

All of the good things about school changed when I was about eleven years old. I got sick; I had rheumatic fever. I don't remember too much about it because I was weak and sleepy all of the time. I ended up spending a year in a sanatorium, a place called Montebello. My brother Lloyd was there too, though I didn't know it for a long time. I ended up getting set back in school because of that year, and after that I just lost interest in school. Maybe it was because all of my friends had been promoted; I don't know. I just wasn't interested anymore.

I went to a vocational high school. Science, woodworking, auto mechanics, and sheet metal were the subjects I liked most. English was the same as always; it just wouldn't sink in. I was on the rifle team for a while, and I enjoyed that. The biggest thing I remember about those years is smoking and drinking in the lavatory.

I was getting tired of Baltimore, too. There wasn't discrimination on the streetcars, but the whole city let you know how they felt about Negroes. There was only one store downtown that we could go in; that was Brager-Eisenberg on Eutaw Street. Even there, when my mother went in to buy a hat, she couldn't try it on. As far as I know, there was only one Negro lawyer. The best jobs in those days were to be a preacher, schoolteacher, mail carrier, or city worker.

Now I had only a week left, and I spent a lot of time thinking. The more I thought, the more I believed that joining the Navy was the answer for me. I just had to come up with a plan in order to leave.

On the twenty-seventh, one day before I had to leave, it came to me: I would get Eddie to help. Now all I had to do was convince him.

"Eddie, I need you to do me a favor. I'll come over in the morning and change here." I passed him the brown paper bag while we sat in his basement listening to records and smoking.

"You gonna be on time?" he asked. "I can't be late anymore; you know I have to be at school earlier than you do."

"Don't worry; I'll be there in plenty of time. Just make sure you don't oversleep."

I got up to leave. On one hand, I felt bad about putting Eddie in the middle of my situation, but I was getting desperate. I could see my chance slipping away, so I had to make my move. I didn't want to tell him any more than I had to; the less he knew, the less he could tell. I would write Eddie a letter and explain everything later. Right now I couldn't take a chance on his accidentally saying something around my parents. As a matter of fact, I didn't trust *me* not to say anything around my parents; that was the biggest reason I had come over to Eddie's house. The tension was driving me nuts. The sooner I could get to the recruiting station, the better.

Eddie opened the door at the top of the stairs. "OK, man, just make sure you're here on time." I left, pulling my coat tighter as I stepped into the air. I wanted my last night at home to be over as soon as possible. On the way I thought about the war, my parents, and Baltimore. I really wasn't worried about the war; I would miss my parents (especially my mother), but I'd get over it; and the city of Baltimore would get along fine without me. I did-n't know how life in the Navy would be, but I was ready to spend my last night under my father's roof.

The next morning, I turned up the collar of my overcoat as I waited for the streetcar. Eddie had already gone to school. I made sure he left first because that way he wouldn't know that I was going downtown. I climbed onto the streetcar, grateful that I didn't have to wait a long time. It was cold, and if I had to wait too long, I might just change my mind. The trip took only twenty minutes, but it seemed like a couple of hours. I thought that I would be feeling a lot of emotion, but the only thing I felt was impatience. When I arrived at the post office it was about ten minutes before eight.

I joined a group of about fifteen other men who were leaving that day. At 8 A.M. an officer took us into a room. His tone was serious as he had us form lines, raise our right hands, and take an oath. He told us that we were offi-cially in the U.S. Navy. We were given meal tickets, which he said were good for breakfast at any downtown restaurant, and were told to be back in one hour. As we left the building, I stopped to look around. There was only one other Negro in the group, and the two of us were left while the white guys walked toward a restaurant in the next block. We knew that no restaurant in downtown Baltimore would serve us, so we tore up the meal tickets and spent the hour walking the streets. We never saw the white guys again.

When we returned to the recruiting station, an officer told me that I was in charge and gave me two manila envelopes. The large one contained our records; the smaller had our traveling instructions, a taxi voucher, and train tickets. We were to go to the naval training station at Great Lakes, Illinois, where I was to give the larger envelope to the officer at the main gate. The recruiting officer took us to the train station, and we boarded the Liberty Limited for Chicago.

2 *Great Lakes*

I was keeping up with the time as the Liberty Limited sped toward Chicago. We had left Baltimore at 9:30 A.M. I wouldn't be missed until about seven in the evening, when my parents would notice that I hadn't returned home from school for dinner. I found myself free of worry for about ten hours. I hadn't felt this way since the first time I walked into the recruiting station in Baltimore. The feeling didn't last long, though. I didn't sleep much that night, once I realized that my parents would become increasingly concerned about me as the hours passed.

We arrived in Chicago early the next morning and took a taxi to another station. There we caught a train that would take us to the naval training station. During this ride it occurred to me that my parents might never find me.

The train stopped in front of the main gate at the naval training station. There was an office at the gate. We went to the office, and I gave the envelope containing our records to an officer inside. He told us to wait for transportation to our camp.

After what seemed like an hour, a Negro sailor came in, said something, and signaled us to come with him. He stopped beside an open-body truck parked out front. He told us to hop onto the back while he got into the cab. As soon as we were all aboard, he pulled off. It was cold as hell, riding on the back of that truck. He drove like he was late for something, and the wind whipped across us, making it even colder. We all ducked as low as we could, trying to avoid the wind. Eventually we straightened up to try to see where we were going.

As we entered the base, all I could see was barracks, barracks, and more barracks. We passed lots of camps. Each camp had a gate with a sign over it. Some of the names were Camp Perry, Camp Moffit, Camp McIntyre, and Camp Lawrence. As we passed each camp, the guards would call out to us. They would yell things like "You're gonna be sorry" or "You had a good home but you left." Their voices stayed with us long after we had passed.

The truck came to a gate marked Camp Robert Smalls; I found out later that the Negro for whom this camp was named had been a Union ship pilot in the Civil War. The driver drove through the gate and stopped in front of a building. The sign over the door read Battalion Headquarters. The driver got out and signaled us to follow him into the building. As we did, I threw my cigarette onto the ground. The driver looked at me, at the cigarette, then at me once more. He smiled knowingly as we entered the office. I didn't know it at the time, but that was the last cigarette I would throw on the ground for a long time. We gathered together, glad to be out of the cold, while the driver took some papers to an officer sitting behind a desk. This officer called a Negro sailor who was standing by a flag in the corner of the office and told him to take us over to Company 151. We left the building and entered the one next to it.

There was a white officer sitting behind a desk in a small room to our left. He got up from the desk and picked up a clipboard from a bed, which was the only other piece of furniture in the room. After looking over the group and making some check marks on a pad on the clipboard, he introduced himself.

"Men, I'm Chief Petty Officer John Shannon, your company commander. Welcome to Great Lakes Naval Training Station and Camp Robert Smalls." His voice was loud and clear, but it didn't seem strained. After the guards who had yelled at the truck as we passed the other camps, Chief Shannon's voice seemed pleasant. He was about six feet tall with a medium build, but his voice sounded like it should have belonged to a much larger man. It was somewhere between bass and baritone, and he had a slight trace of a Southern accent. If he was from the South, he must've been gone a long time, since he had almost lost his accent.

"You men are assigned to Company 151. We are not yet up to our full complement. We must be at full strength in order to begin our training program. Until that time you are not to leave the building unless I tell you. When you do go outside, the smoking lamp will be off. That means that there will be no smoking. The only time that smoking is permitted is when I tell you that the smoking lamp is lit. If you are not sure what my last instruction was, the smart thing to do is not to smoke." Even though the tone of his voice hadn't changed, Chief Shannon didn't seem so pleasant anymore.

"As I said, the training program will commence as soon as the company is at its full complement. At that time you will receive clothing and bedding. You are assigned to the second platoon, so follow Seaman Smith to the second floor."

Having said all that he had planned to say, he made a few more marks on his clipboard and went back into his office. I got the impression that, like my father, he was used to saying things one time and having his instructions followed. I reminded myself that I had joined the Navy to get away from my father and his rules.

Camp Robert Smalls was run very efficiently. The training program lasted sixteen weeks. There were sixteen companies training at any given time. Each week one company completed training while a new company was being formed. Of the sixteen company commanders, fifteen were white. The one Negro was named Lear. His rating was first-class petty officer, while the white company commanders were chief petty officers.

As Chief Shannon had told us, our company was not at its full complement. As men arrived, they would be assigned to their barracks one floor at a time. One floor—sixty men—made up one platoon. Once the first floor was full, men would be assigned to the second floor. When all spaces on the second floor had been filled, the company was complete, and training could begin.

We followed Seaman Smith to the second floor. It was different from any building I had ever seen. As you entered, there was a rectangular partition on each side of the door. The partition, which was about four and a half feet high, was made of five-inch steel piping. Each partition was divided into six smaller sections. I found out that in the Navy this was known as a jackstay. Five men slept in each of the smaller sections of each jackstay, called a bay, which meant that sixty men slept on each floor. What made the situation even more interesting was that we were to sleep in hammocks. I didn't even know what a hammock was.

Now I had a chance to look around at the men who were going to make up this company. This was the first time I had really paid attention to the other men in the group, and believe me, I had only sympathy for some of them. This camp was the only one in the United States that was training men to carry out President Roosevelt's order to integrate the Navy. You could tell what part of the country these men came from by the way they were dressed. The men from the Deep South had on pants or coveralls and shirts; the men from the West had on suits or sports clothes; and the men from the cold areas in the North had on suits or sports clothes too, plus overcoats or top coats.

I was glad that I had winter clothes because I don't believe there are many places in the United States that get colder than the Great Lakes area in the winter. When we went to chow, those guys from the Deep South really suffered. I found out that some of them were wearing all of the clothes they had. That was a real shock to me, since I had always liked to wear nice clothes and always paid attention to how I was dressed. I had never thought of myself as well off, but after seeing those guys, I had a new understanding of what being poor meant.

We arrived at Great Lakes on a Friday. That night we found ourselves praying that the company would be complete soon, because until we got our bedding, we would have to sleep on the floor. I had always taken a warm bed for granted, but that weekend I found out just how important a mattress and blankets were. The floor was my mattress, and my overcoat was my blanket. Friday night when I lay down, wrapped in my overcoat, I had to shiver myself to sleep. I felt every board in the floor; they seemed to cut right into my back. I eventually settled for rolling halfway onto my side. Even though my overcoat came only to my knees, and being on my side rolled the coat up enough to let a draft come across my hips and back, at least I was able to take the pressure off my back. I woke up three times during the night, and I had to force myself back onto the hard wood each time, but I couldn't complain. Every time I woke up, I'd look at the guy to my left. I didn't know his name, but I think he was from Mississippi; I remember that he had a Southern accent and wore only a pair of coveralls and a thin shirt. When I woke up Saturday morning, my back was stiff, and I was already dreading another night on the floor. Saturday night was worse than Friday, because even before I lay down my body remembered how the floor felt.

Sunday morning Chief Shannon called us down to the first floor and announced that enough men would be coming that day to fill out our company. We would be ready to begin our training on Monday. It took a while for us to understand what he was really saying. If training started tomorrow, that meant that we would receive our clothing and bedding on Monday! We would have only one more night of sleeping on the floor! The time couldn't go by fast enough. I looked forward to that night because it would be my last on that hard, cold floor.

On Monday we boarded trucks to ride to a neighboring camp for our final physical examination, our clothing allotment, and our dog tags. Dog tags were your identification. They were supposed to be worn on a chain around your neck at all times. They were engraved with your name, service number, blood type, religion, and race. This information would be used to identify bodies of people who were killed in action.

I thought I'd had a thorough physical examination at the Navy recruiting station in Baltimore, but the one we were given at Great Lakes was more detailed. This exam was conducted so efficiently that we lost four or five of our company. They almost lost me too, for at the end of the examination a Navy corpsman stamped into my service record "Qualified for Submarine Duty." That phrase the guards had yelled—"You had a good home but you left"—was beginning to have some meaning. I had volunteered to integrate the Navy on top of the water, not under it. The idea of going down in a submarine had me nervous. I thought maybe I should have a talk with President Roosevelt about this. I was relieved five minutes later when I was told that in order to get into the submarine service, I would have to volunteer. There was no way that was going to happen!

They measured my feet, and now for the first time I was wearing the correct size. All this time, I had been wearing shoes too small.

I soon learned that in the military there were two sides to everything, even good news. It was great that we didn't have to sleep on the floor anymore, but the surprise was that we had to sleep in hammocks. That first night was really an experience of a lifetime. Our trainers showed us how to lace a hammock and how to draw it tight to the jackstay. You put your mattress and pillow in the hammock; that was the easy part. The hard part was getting into the hammock and staying there. Bodies were hitting the floor for a week. One soon learns to lie still in a hammock.

Our training started with three days of testing. After these tests the Navy knew more about my abilities than I knew myself. This testing had me thinking that I could have accomplished anything if only I had finished high school!

Now, there was a word used in boot camp: *motherfucka*. I had never heard the word before, so I know it didn't originate in Baltimore. You were a motherfucka when you got up, and you were a motherfucka all day. You were a motherfucka when you went to sleep, and you were a motherfucka while you slept. This was every day!

Chief Shannon took us out onto the drill field with the seemingly impossible task of teaching us the correct way to march. There was no doubt in my mind that Shannon had days when he wished that he were on board ship fighting the enemy rather than in this boot camp trying to teach us to march.

Early in boot camp you learn that the Navy has various types of disciplinary action. The punishment is determined by the offense. You might have to stand on a bucket out in the snow for an hour or two. You might have to go down to the drill hall and hold a rifle in front of you, shoulder high, until your arms felt like they were going to fall off. Or your platoon or your whole company might be ordered out onto the drill field with all your gear lashed up in seagoing fashion and marched around the drill field till you were ready to drop. There was also the "Slagger Squad," the last step before being kicked out of the Navy. You had to do something really bad to be put on the Slagger Squad. The guys on the Slagger Squad worked twenty out of twenty-four hours a day, and the things they did weren't easy. They always did the hardest, dirtiest, and toughest work in the camp.

After we had been in training for about three weeks, I found out about another type of discipline. Each morning we had to march down to the drill hall for personal inspection. Here each trainee was inspected to see if he had shaved, bathed, put on clean underwear, and pressed his uniform. Since we had no irons, we kept our uniforms pressed by putting them under the mattress and sleeping on them.

On this day I decided that my underwear was clean enough to pass inspection, so I didn't change it. The inspecting officer stopped in front of me, grabbed the collar of my T-shirt, turned it inside out, and asked my name. As soon as he asked, I knew that I was on report. I hadn't thought it was that big a deal; I had thought I was clean enough. Hell, I was used to taking a bath just once a week.

When we returned to the dorm the whole platoon took off their clothes. Each man had a clothes brush, the type used to scrub clothes. They took me into the shower and began to scrub each piece of clothing I had on. When they finished that, they scrubbed me. I was red for two days, but I was never caught in inspection again.

Every Wednesday night during my training at Great Lakes, we had what is known in the Navy as the Happy Hour. This was when all sixteen companies assembled in the enormous drill hall to see shows. These shows were put on by the USO or by trainees in the camp. During the shows put on by the camp, the admiral commanding Great Lakes Naval Training Station would speak to us. He was the first one to tell us that we had to be "better than good."

The admiral explained that there were no guidelines for us to follow in integrating the Navy. This was the first time anything like this had been attempted in the history of our country, and there was absolutely nothing to guide us; the only thing he could tell us was to use our heads. He warned us of the certainty of hostilities from the white personnel of the Navy, both officers and enlisted men. He said that it was not going to be at all pleasant, but this we must face. It was up to us to find ways to overcome the obstacles. He said the only way he could think of was for us to study hard in the various schools that the Navy was sending us to. But whether we got sent to specialized schools or not, we must perform our duties to the best of our abilities. Above all, we had to use our heads, and we had to be "better than good" in order to compete with white sailors. He made one point very plain: We must at all times abide by the Articles of War and the rules and regulations governing the U.S. Navy. If we violated these rules, we would receive no special treatment.

This admiral spoke to us on several occasions, and each time he hammered "better than good" into our heads; just being good was not good enough; we had to be "better than good." He was not the only officer to address us. We were never addressed by an officer below the rank of commander. We were never addressed by a civilian while at Great Lakes. The only Negro to address us was the naval hero of Pearl Harbor, Dorie Miller.

At every Happy Hour we sang the Navy anthem. There are a lot of Navy men who have never heard it. The words are:

Stand uncovered men in blue
Stand with hearts so brave and true
Sing to shipmates on the sea
Valiant warriors of the free
Let the voice of freedom rise
Over land, sea, and skies
Triumphantly in tribute to
Those valiant men in blue.

There was a boy among us who once sang the anthem and held the last word, *blue,* too long, and he was put on the Slagger Squad for a week.

Chief Shannon brought us along in our training program. One day he took us over to the swimming pool for a life-jacket drill. This drill was performed from an elevated platform above the pool. Whether you could swim or not, you had to go off the platform. The most commonly used life jacket in the Navy was the Mae West, a vest type that used cork as the flotation element. You couldn't just put on this jacket and jump. To do it properly, you had to tie the straps across your body, then fasten the two straps that came through the legs. When jumping, you had to grab the jacket under your chin and pull down as hard as you could till you hit the water, feet first. If this wasn't done properly, the jacket would come up and hit you in the chin.

Shannon showed a lot of patience with us. He never got angry enough to cuss anyone, but he made it clear that he meant what he said. He proved this to us by the manner in which he administered discipline. Whenever one member of the company did something wrong, the entire company was punished. This had two purposes: to demonstrate that one man could foul up a ship, and to teach the importance of teamwork.

We sang many songs as we marched. One was "You had a good home but you left / You're right." Other favorites were "There's no need to worry your head / Jody's in your big brass bed" and "Eyes right, assholes tight,

ankles to the rear / We are men of the U.S. Navy and we all got gonorrhea."
These songs would keep us in step and help to take our minds off the fact
that we were marching, but my mother would have had a fit if she had heard
me singing some of this stuff.

There was another thing we did at Great Lakes: the Great Lakes Shuf-
fle. You put a ball of steel wool under each foot and cleaned the hardwood
floor. The floor was then waxed and buffed. No shoes were allowed in the
dorm from Friday evening till after inspection on Saturday.

Two or three nights a week Chief Shannon would call the company
together on one floor and go over some of the various things we needed
to know. Sometimes he would read the Articles of War and the rules and
regulations of the U.S. Navy; he might teach us to tie various knots or
demonstrate how to salute properly; but he never said one word to us
about our purpose.

One Sunday I got a message that I had a visitor at the canteen. I could-
n't think of anyone who would be visiting me at Great Lakes. I was sure it
was a mistake, but I went anyhow. It was my brother Lloyd, who was a lieutenant in the Army. Except for the times when we had speakers come to
the unit, we rarely saw naval officers in our area. Most of these guys had
never even seen an Army officer, and Lloyd was sharp! He was decked out
in full uniform, down to the Sam Browne belt. I guess he must have caught
a ride somehow, because our area was about two miles from the main gate,
and his boots were shining like new money. He was really something to see,
because wherever he went, everyone hurried to get out of his way. I was
really glad to see him. We talked for a while, mostly catching up on the family. Of course he was more up to date on everything than I was. We sat
around for about an hour, then he left. I never did learn how he found me,
but he sure was a sight for sore eyes.

Near the end of the sixteen weeks at Great Lakes I found out that I was
not the only person in the company who had run away to join the Navy. In
training there is a person called the guide who marches in front of the platoon, carrying the company banner. Our guide was from South Carolina,
and his mother finally wrote the Navy to inform them that he was thirteen
years old. He had gotten a friend to sign his mother's name on his enlistment papers. There was no way that the Navy was going to intercede for
him; they found him guilty of being a stowaway, and he was sent home. The
worst part about it was that training was over, and he had gone all the way

through boot camp for nothing. He was a tough little guy, though. He swore that he would be back as soon as he was old enough. The commanding officer of the camp said that he would be welcome. I thought that I had been in a bad situation, but I couldn't even imagine what this guy's situation was like.

Graduation day in a boot camp is very emotional. Our ceremony took place in the drill hall. This was the last time our company would march together. The whole battalion paraded before the admiral. Chief Shannon sweated it out as we went through our paces a final time. The whole battalion started at right shoulder arms. Commands echoed from battalion, to company, to platoon. At the command "Order arms," a thousand rifle butts simultaneously hit the floor with a resounding BOOM! As the ceremony ended we sang the battle hymn "Onward Christian Soldiers" while marching in formation. I was so excited that I could have walked right out of that drill hall into Tokyo and ended this war right then. At least that's how I felt at the time.

Chief Shannon marched us out onto the drill field and brought us to a halt. He told us that our training at Great Lakes was completed, and we were now sailors in the U.S. Navy. He then instructed us to remove the boots we had worn for the past sixteen weeks. As soon as I removed my boots, I lit a cigarette—the first I had been permitted to smoke outside of a building since I arrived at Great Lakes sixteen weeks before. Later that day we went to another camp to get paid. We each received four months' pay at the rate of $21 a month. We stored our gear in a storeroom, then Chief Shannon took us to the train station. I was homeward bound for nine days' leave.

The train ride home was a lot different from the trip to boot camp. Even though it had been only four months, a lot had happened. I definitely wasn't the same person who had slipped away from Baltimore at the end of January. Life at home was different. Most of the people I ran into didn't know I had joined the Navy. A few of the guys in the neighborhood had joined the service while I was in boot camp, but most of the gang was still around. Everyone made remarks about how good I looked in uniform, and I didn't have to pay for drinks the whole time I was home. Some new records had come out. I heard "C. C. Rider" by B.B. Booze for the first time, and everybody else was calling it an old record.

The house was pretty much the same. My parents didn't treat me any differently, but they seemed to be glad to see me. My room was just the same as I had left it. I learned that I could sleep in my bed all night and only leave one wrinkle; I was so accustomed to sleeping in a hammock that I stayed in one position the whole night. My father didn't make turtle soup the whole time I was home, and I was grateful for that. All of my brothers were still away in the service. They were all in different branches: Lloyd was in the infantry, Ellsworth was a medic, and Vernon was in the Air Force; even my brother-in-law Walter was in the coast artillery. Since they weren't home, we never got the chance to disagree over which branch was better. I found out that my father, who was the youngest son of his parents, had run away and gone to sea, too. I planned to go to sea; that was the biggest reason I joined the Navy. I had more in common with my father than I previously thought.

Nine days was not a long time for visiting relatives and catching up with the guys and girls. Before I knew it, my leave was over, and I had to go back to Great Lakes.

The return to Camp Robert Smalls was quite different from my first arrival. There were no calls of "You're gonna be sorry" or "You had a good home but you left." I wasn't sorry that I had joined the Navy; in fact, I was happy about the whole thing. Each day that I had been in the Navy had been a new experience for me, and I had enjoyed it.

I was assigned to the outgoing unit to wait for transfer to the United States Navy Service School at Hampton Institute in Hampton, Virginia. I was going to be trained as a motor machinist; the course was sixteen weeks. I had dreamed of attending Hampton Institute for some years. This dream had been abandoned after I lost interest in school, and especially because my parents couldn't afford to pay for me to go there. Now the Navy was sending me there to study. I was lucky; the guys who got sent to base companies remained in the same company until they got out of the Navy, and they only worked in service areas. Enlisting in the Navy seemed to have been the smartest move of my young life.

Each month the Navy sent a company of men to Hampton Institute to study various courses. Students for the service school were selected from the training companies. It would take a few weeks to get enough men to form a service-school company. While I was waiting for the company to form, I had numerous opportunities to go into Chicago.

Chicago! I had heard a lot of songs and stories about that place. Chicago was a Northern city, and the Negroes there were supposedly free to go wherever they chose and to live where they wanted, and they supposedly lived better than the Negroes in the South. I really believed these things as I entered the city. I felt free to go anywhere; at first I felt far removed from the segregation that I had known at home. But I soon learned that Negroes in Chicago lived in one section, on the South Side. Most of them lived in dilapidated wooden-frame houses, and when the wind blows on South Park, the littered main street of that section, you can hardly see for all the trash blowing around. So this is the Windy City, I thought; here is where the Southern Negro comes to escape the humiliating segregation of the South. From what I could see with my own eyes, I knew that this escape was only in these people's minds, for in reality they were still as segregated as they ever were. In my travels around Chicago, this great Northern city, I never saw any noticeable mixing of the races. There was one USO for Negroes and another one for whites. As I left the city, I couldn't help thinking that my home in Baltimore was a lot better.

By the middle of May the company that was to go to Hampton Institute had formed. We finally boarded a train for our new base. The Navy made certain that we were not subjected to any segregation on the trains as we went south. We had the last cars on the train, not those next to the engine where Negroes traveling south usually had to ride. The trip was pleasant.

The author in California, 1944

Company 151, U.S. Naval Training Station, Great Lakes, Illinois, 1943

SHANNON – C.S.P. CO. COM'D. MAR 9, 1943.
...NING STATION – GREAT LAKES, ILL.

Mole

The author and fellow sailors at Hampton on work detail

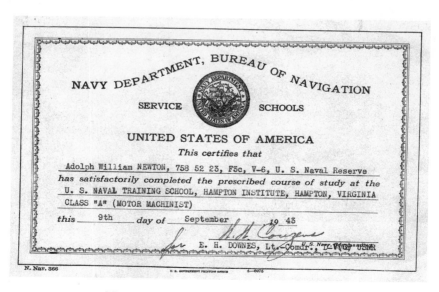

Newton's Hampton Institute certificate

Seamen, Camp Robert Smalls, Great Lakes Naval Station
Courtesy James W. Graham

Gunnery school, Camp Robert Smalls, Great Lakes Naval Station
Courtesy James W. Graham

Signalman's school, Camp Robert Smalls, Great Lakes Naval Station
Courtesy James W. Graham

Inspection, Camp Robert Smalls, Great Lakes Naval Station
Courtesy James W. Graham

USS *Donner*
U.S. Naval Institute

3 *Hampton*

Despite its small size, the Hampton area has naval and historical significance. The first battle between ironclad naval vessels—the *Monitor* and the *Merrimac*—occurred in Hampton Roads, the body of water that separates Hampton from Norfolk. There is a fort in Hampton, Fort Monroe, which belongs to the U.S. Army. During the Civil War the fort was considered Union territory, so any slave who made it there was considered free. Norfolk was home to one of the largest naval bases on the East Coast, and the cities of Norfolk, Portsmouth, and Newport News had some of the largest shipyards in the country.

Unaware of this history, we disembarked from the train in the little town of Hampton and marched to the campus of Hampton Institute, a very important institution in Negro history. This was where Booker T. Washington, the founder of Tuskegee Institute, had been educated. Hampton Institute enjoyed a reputation as one of the top Negro colleges in the country. There were no male students on the campus as residents, because the Navy had taken over all the male dormitories except one, which was being used by the Army. A multitude of girls lined our route.

We were told that these young ladies were there to study and that we were not to molest them in any way. Anyone who did would be kicked out of service school, maybe out of the Navy, depending upon the offense. We took these warnings very seriously. Nobody got into trouble concerning any of those college girls while I was there.

The people of Hampton were so pleased that the Navy had chosen Hampton Institute as a service school that they gave all Navy personnel stationed there the key to the town. This meant that we Negro sailors, wearing the gold service-school *S* on our uniforms, could go anywhere in the town. This freedom applied only to Navy personnel, and not to Negroes who lived in Hampton. We sailors did not feel bad about this; at least the people of Hampton were making a step in the right direction. We thought that if we made a good showing, these opportunities might be extended to include Negroes who lived there. The Negro residents never had any problems when we were with them.

The service school at Hampton was considered a "Class A" school. It had opened in September 1942, so it had been in operation for a little more than six months when I arrived. The courses taught were electricity, forging and welding, diesel engineering, carpentry, shipfitting, and motor machinist, which was the course I would be taking. A motor machinist handled the operation, maintenance, and overhaul of gasoline- and diesel-fueled engines, as well as steam propulsion, refrigeration, electricity, and the operation of lathes and drill presses.

It is a reflection on the instructors and the school that only one person failed to complete this sixteen-week course while my company was there. I should point out that this was the guy who got blown through the deck of a PT boat in an explosion. We never found out what he had been doing down there to cause the explosion, but he was lucky to be alive. Other than him, everybody who was at the service school while I was there graduated from the course.

Our days in the service school were busy. Our first morning classes were makeup, which was basic educational skills, like reading and writing. The rest of the morning was devoted to math classes and theory. Theory dealt with how engines worked. Afternoons were spent in the machine shop actually working on the engines. The last period of every day before dinner was GI, which was another name for cleaning up. GI was taken very seriously, because there were inspections every Saturday. Liberty for the weekend depended on how we did at the captain's inspection. Every night from eight until ten-thirty we had study hall, which was also taken very seriously. Everyone knew that each day's work was the foundation for what would be covered the following day, and no one wanted to be caught short.

The Navy paid attention to our physical fitness, too. There was a lot of physical training: boxing, wrestling, basketball, and swimming. The Navy had a swimming pool and gym built for us. They worked out an agreement with the school so that students could use these facilities when we weren't using them. Some other activities provided for us were the rifle team, the glee club, and Happy Hour. We had a Happy Hour program every Wednesday evening. The first part would be a religious service. There would be music by the glee club, and sometimes other trainees would perform. The second part of the program might be something of special interest; many times we had guest speakers.

An important aspect of our training at Hampton Institute was boat handling. There was a white chief boatswain's mate in charge, and he was tough. He was the meanest white man I have ever met. When we continually messed up on something he told us to do, he would hang his foot in our pants. He chewed tobacco, and his every second word was a cuss word. This chief had been in the Navy for over twenty years, and he let it be known that he was the boss in the boathouse. He had us afraid of him. When he took us out for sailing instructions on windy days, he would spit into the wind. That tobacco juice would fly all over our white uniforms. He said that he had been around the Horn and had the right to spit into the wind. On these sailing trips I had an earnest wish that the Navy would place me on a ship going around the Horn and let me come back to meet this chief on a windy day. When we were about to leave Hampton we learned that he had been ordered to be extra hard on us so that we would know what to expect later. The last I saw of him was at Hampton Institute. He was still raising hell.

There was only one Negro civilian who had anything to do with our training: the music instructor for Hampton Institute, Mr. Flax. He trained and directed the service-school choir and was in charge of our Happy Hour. At the end of our training he gave us a speech. He said that we were heading for destinations unknown, and the only thing he could say to help us was whatever we did, for God's sake, use our heads.

General Benjamin Davis came to inspect us one Friday. Benjamin Davis was the only Negro general in the U.S. Army. That Thursday, after class, everybody reported to the dorm. Windows were washed; every corner, light bulb, and wall was cleaned. The floors were steel-wooled, waxed, and polished. Every bed was taken was apart and cleaned; each bedspring was taken into the shower and scrubbed. The school commander sent a truckload of Coca-Cola and had it parked at the front door. If you wanted something to drink, you just went to the front door and got it. After 9 P.M. no shoes were worn in the dorm. We worked till 1 A.M., then went to bed.

The next day General Davis inspected us in formation, then put on white gloves and went into the building. After an hour, he and the school commander came out. The commander said that the general had found some dust in one spot: inside the fuse box. He wouldn't find it there next time.

The week before our training at Hampton was over, the whole company was given a seventy-two-hour pass to Washington, D.C. Once again we were put in cars at the end of a train and were told the time the train would leave Washington to return to Hampton.

When we got to Washington, a lot of us went to a bar. About six of us were sitting at a table when a girl came up to us.

"I've been looking for you!" she said.

We all looked at each other.

"All of you," she said.

Now we were *really* looking at each other.

"I have some girlfriends, and we want to party. We got the food and drinks."

We got into a couple of cabs and went with her.

She was right: there was an acute shortage of men at this party, and all the women, food, and drinks one man could handle. I stayed from Friday evening till Saturday evening; I was the only one to leave. I went to Baltimore for a while but returned to Washington in time to catch the train. The guys who had stayed at the party said they needed a couple of weeks to rest.

At our last formation at Hampton, the commanding officer of the service school spoke to us. He said that because many of us wanted to remain on the East Coast but only six of the whole company could stay, we would draw slips. The slips would have the names of our destinations on them; this way there would be no favoritism. He wished us luck. I drew the U.S. Naval Frontier Base, San Diego, California.

4 *Frontier Base*

Once again I was on a train. We had a four-hour layover in Chicago and went to some parties arranged by some fellows with us who lived there. We drank and danced for about three hours and returned to the train station with armloads of whiskey. We had another party there in the station.

I don't know how long it took our train to go from Chicago to Los Angeles, but there is a commercial train that runs from Los Angeles to Chicago called the El Capitan. The El Capitan makes the trip in thirty-nine hours, and there is only one train. This train passed us three times on our way to Los Angeles, so I know we didn't break any speed records.

After Chicago, our next stop was Kansas City. I was very anxious to see this place, since I was a jazz fan, and Kansas City was important in the jazz world. Every big city has its famous streets; Kansas City's famous place is Eighteenth and Vine. I personally saw nothing on this corner to sing about. The homes were all frame houses, and most were

27

painted gray. I was disappointed, and was glad when it was time to go back to the train.

We returned to find that two cars of Waves (female sailors) had been hooked on to our train. These Waves created a lot of excitement and ideas on our part, but the ideas immediately went out of the window. These Waves were white, and the Navy had sent Shore Patrolmen to protect them. In spite of that, we still had some fun. Whenever the train stopped, they would march past our cars and we would give them bottles of whiskey. The train stopped every five or six hours, so this really helped us pass the time.

The Navy was in no rush to get us to California. We didn't have a dining car on the train, so we had to stop for meals. The meals were the same each day wherever we stopped: breakfast, lunch, and dinner, it was the same thing every day, prepared Mexican-style. After the fourth day, nobody had much of an appetite.

We arrived in Los Angeles broke, dirty, hungry, and tired—California, the land of sunshine and orange trees growing in everyone's yard. Here in the Los Angeles train station, our group split up. It would be the last time many of us would see each other. The largest draft of men was going to the Frontier Base in San Diego. We boarded our respective trains and departed.

After arriving in San Diego we boarded buses for the Frontier Base. As we were riding to the base, we entered a shaded area. Looking up, we saw to our surprise that we were riding under a gigantic net that stretched over the buildings. This net, which covered a great portion of the city, hid one of our large aircraft assembly plants. From the sea or air the city looked like a large farm area, complete with houses and cattle, while in reality it was full of sailors and Marines.

Frontier Base was nestled at the base of a hill on a point jutting out into the ocean called Point Loma. Not a very large base, Frontier Base handled only small patrol craft, which operated out past San Clemente. This base also operated the antisubmarine nets that protected the San Diego harbor. The personnel on this base were about 70 percent Negro. The Negro sailors had a large dormitory, and the whites had a much smaller one.

I think my troubles really started upon my arrival at the base in San Diego. I found out on the trip from Hampton that my sea bag with all my clothes in it had been lost. All I had was a dress uniform, a set of dungarees, and three pairs of underwear. The Navy would not replace my lost gear.

At that time a complete issue cost over $200, and I was making $50 a month. It would be many months before I replaced most of my gear; I never replaced it all.

The first thing I did was to ask some of the Negro sailors what life was like for Negroes in San Diego. They said that it "wasn't shit"; they called San Diego "Little Georgia." I went into town and found that they had told the truth. As I walked around the main street I saw signs in almost every window with the words "No Colored Allowed." A sign in one window said "No Sailors, Dogs, or Colored Allowed." There were only about five places that Negroes could go in San Diego. These places were not worth the print it takes to mention them, but as I said, there was nowhere else to go.

One spot in San Diego where we hung out was called the Silver Slipper. Two small groups played there. One was the King Cole Trio (the leader was better known as Nat King Cole); the other was Illinois Jacquet and his band. After King Cole and his trio recorded "Straighten Up and Fly Right," he left San Diego.

One morning when I had been on the base for about a week I was walking from the dormitory to the motor machinist shop, to which I was assigned. I heard someone calling, "Nigger, here nigger, come here nigger." I was thinking, *Who in the hell is that?* and I turned around. To my astonishment, about thirty feet from me was a four-striper captain who continued to call out, "Nigger, here nigger." I stood there and looked at him; all I could do was stare. Tears began to run down my cheeks. I said to myself, *The nerve of this son of a bitch.* I had, up to now, had the utmost respect for all officers of the Navy, but this was ridiculous. To really add to the insult, a coal-black dog ran up to him. I was so mad that I spun around and walked away in disgust.

I was still angry when I got to the shop. "Did you guys know there's a captain on this base that calls his dog Nigger?"

The guys looked at each other. One of the older guys said softly, "Newt, that's the base commander."

I couldn't believe my ears. "You guys let him get away with that? How can you let that happen?"

"What the hell can we do about it? Think, man. Who can we report him to?"

"You're right about that. He runs this base, so his word is law. But damn, there ought to be something we could do. If we can't do anything else, we could kill that little bastard of a dog."

"Don't think that you're the first one to come up with that idea. Ain't nobody crazy enough to kill the captain's dog. That's a guaranteed court-martial. 'Sides, ain't nobody been able to catch the damn thing."

The tension in the room eased as everyone laughed. Now and then this dog would come into the shop. People would throw anything they could get their hands on at the dog, and sometimes somebody would hit him. The shop officers would come into the shop, and everyone would play dumb.

About a month after I arrived on the Frontier Base, I was put on kitchen police duty and assigned to the spud locker. This was the best duty on KP because everyone had liberty each night, and every other weekend half of us had a seventy-two-hour pass.

Fourteen miles to the south of San Diego lay the Mexican border and the town of Tijuana. This was where I went with four other sailors from the base on my first weekend pass. Tijuana was a dingy and dilapidated little town with houses made of wood. The city in no way resembled the Mexico that I had pictured.

As we walked around Tijuana I came to the conclusion that there were only three types of buildings in this town. One sold whiskey cheaper than in the United States, which was odd considering the fact that the whiskey was made in the States. The second type sold souvenirs, and the third were brothels. I really can't say which of the three was busiest.

Little kids were always present, running around the streets. One came up to us and said, "Hey, Joe, you want to meet a nice girl, Joe? Come with me, Joe, and I will take you to meet my sister." We followed one ten-year-old "nookie bookie" to a house where I thought I was going to have my first affair with a Mexican girl but ended up having my first with a white American girl. I didn't know anything about this girl, but I believe she couldn't have come from any place but Texas. Everything is big in Texas.

Now, the armed services were having various major troubles at this time, and one of these troubles was venereal disease. The U.S. Navy, in an all-out effort to combat the problem, came up with the idea of charging personnel who contracted a venereal disease with misconduct, and the man would forfeit his pay during the period of hospitalization. This stopped nothing; the venereal disease wards stayed full.

The general procedure when a person contracted a venereal disease was that he would be turned in to the sick bay or hospital and put in the Clap Shack (the venereal disease ward). During the period of his hospitalization, which at this time was on the average of fourteen days, he would be treated with sulfathiazole and other drugs, and upon being cured, he would be released. This was the normal procedure, but it was not to be the case in my situation.

On the Monday morning following the weekend I had visited Tijuana, I reported to the sick bay, along with all of the men on KP. This was a daily routine during which each individual was checked for cleanliness, making sure that each one had his fingernails clipped short, and each one was given a short-arm (penis) inspection to guard against venereal disease. Being suspicious, the hospital corpsman ordered a smear test on me—"just to be certain," he said. I was detained, pending the outcome of the smear test, which proved positive.

The doctor asked me if I wanted to go over to the naval hospital at Balboa Park and volunteer to use a new drug called penicillin. He said that the treatment would be much shorter than the fourteen-day treatment then being used. I told that doctor that I didn't want to try the new drug. There is a well-known rule among servicemen: Don't volunteer for *nothing*.

The fourteen days went very slowly. All we could drink was milk and water, and we took pills by the hundreds. During this time I was informed that since I had been on KP when I contacted this venereal disease, I would have to go to captain's mast, which was a form of hearing.

When I was released from sick bay, I was also taken off KP. I returned to the motor machinist shop and was assigned to overhaul an engine on a minesweeper. My job was to get inside the sump (oil pan) and clean the inside and around the crankshaft. This was a dirty job, but a necessary one. It was usually given to the lowest-rated man on the overhaul, and I understood that; I had the lowest rate (one can be fireman third class in the motor machinist rating), so I got the job, and I liked it. I enjoyed working on engines, and this one I could really get into. I guess the fact that the engine was so large made the job interesting.

When the bugle blew for lunch, we stopped work, washed up, and went to the mess hall for lunch. When I got up to the door, the master-at-arms stopped me.

"You can't come in here like that!" he said, pointing at me.

I didn't like his tone of voice, plus I didn't like him anyway. As a matter of fact, nobody liked him. "Like what?" I shouted. I wanted him to know I didn't appreciate the way he was talking to me.

"You can't come into my mess hall with all that oil on you. It's that simple."

"Look, it's lunchtime. I don't have time to go change clothes, plus I'm gonna be back working on the same engine just as soon as I get done eating."

"I don't care what you have to do. That's your problem, not mine. You are not coming in this mess hall looking like that."

"You're chickenshit, and you know it."

"What's your name, sailor?" He pulled a pad and pen from the breast pocket of his uniform.

"Newton, Adolph W. Newton. Do you need me to spell it for you?" I turned and started to walk away. There were a lot of things I wanted to say, but I didn't want to get into any more trouble.

"Naw, that's OK, Newton. I can spell it just fine. I hope you can spell *report*, because that's what you're on."

I just kept walking without saying anything. Now I had another reason to go to captain's mast. I didn't have to look for trouble; it always knew where to find me.

The next day, I was up for captain's mast. This was my first experience with military justice. When I entered the office and reported to the captain, he lit right into me.

"Newton, you knowingly were on KP while you had a venereal disease. That's a violation of—"

"Sir, I didn't—"

He slammed his hand onto the desk. "Sailor, never interrupt me while I'm talking! As I was saying, you worked on KP while you knew you had a venereal disease, which is a violation. What do you have to say for yourself?"

"Sir, I didn't know I had anything. The corpsman didn't think I had it at first, either. He said he was giving me a routine smear test."

"Newton, you're a liar. You knew what you had. Because of that, and because of the fact that you called my master-at-arms 'chickenshit,' I'm giving you a summary court-martial. You are restricted to base until your court-martial date."

I had been in the Navy for only about nine months, and I was already getting a summary court-martial. I knew nothing about courts-martial. Even if I had, it wouldn't have changed anything that happened.

The procedures for discipline in the Navy are the most unjust that I have ever encountered. When an enlisted man violates Navy rules and regulations, the first step is to go to captain's mast. At that point the commanding officer decides the action to be taken, if any. In my case I received a summary court-martial.

The next step that occurs is the assignment of a commissioned officer to act as the defense attorney. Generally this officer knows as little about Navy law as the defendant does. He knows even less about the incident involved, because at least the defendant knows what happened. This officer is given a stack of books on U.S. Navy rules and regulations and court-martial procedures, and any other books necessary to create the illusion of presenting an honest defense. The commanding officer then selects four or five commissioned officers (generally from his command) to act as the court, who draw up the charges against the defendant and present the case. The highest-ranking officer of the group presides over the court. There are a few problems with this way of handling things: these officers eat, work, and in some cases drink together; they may share quarters; they are in daily contact with the commanding officer. With all this interaction, it is highly improbable that these officers can hold a fair and just court-martial. It is more likely that they all will agree to whatever the commanding officer wants.

The Navy has three different levels of court-martial: deck, summary, and general. The summary and the general are the only ones that can imprison a person and/or discharge him from the service. Since the possible punishments are so severe, anyone given a summary or general court-martial should have the services of an attorney with training in naval law and procedures. Each Navy district should have a court with trained defense attorneys to try all summary courts-martial in that district.

At my court-martial I received thirty days in the brig, loss of pay for thirty days, and ten days on bread and water. The ten days on bread and water was included in the thirty days in the brig. I had plenty of time to think while I was in the brig, and I came to the conclusion that white girls are expensive. The next time I went to Mexico, I was going to stick to the Mexicans.

When I got out of the brig and went back to the motor machinist shop, I was placed aboard a yard net gate-tender (YNG). The job of a YNG was to open and close the antisubmarine net that protected the harbor of San Diego. This YNG didn't go anywhere; it was anchored to the shore. My job was to operate and maintain the generators that operated the nets. While assigned to this YNG, I became fireman second class.

I learned a lot during this assignment: how to use the sonar that detected submarines, how submarine nets worked, and how to switch the generators. I may not have learned enough about switching generators, though. It is a fast operation. One day I was a little slow doing it and reversed the polarity of the engines. This made the engines run backward, and I shut them off. I told my division officer what had happened, and shortly after that I was sent back to the shop.

One day we were playing basketball when the word came over the PA (public address) system for seven guys to report to the personnel office. They returned saying that they were going to become commissioned officers in the U.S. Navy. We didn't believe them, but it turned out to be true. Shortly after that, they left for officers' school, and I never saw any of them again.

There were a number of fellows on this base that I had been with since I was in boot camp at Great Lakes. One of these guys, named Fleet, from Washington, D.C., was very light-skinned. If you didn't already know that he was a Negro, you would not have been able to tell it from his appearance. He could pass for white anytime he chose, and in San Diego there were times when he did. We went into San Diego together many times. Sometimes Fleet would go into one of those places with a "No Colored Allowed" sign in the window. He would order something or play around with the white girls inside, and I would stand outside and laugh. People who saw me standing out there laughing probably thought I was nuts. What made me laugh was that these white people didn't know a Negro when they saw one. It is said that thousands of Negroes like my friend cross over into the white race every year undetected. They marry white men and women and have children, and everyone is happy. When these people who "pass" come face to face with another Negro, they become uneasy. They fear being exposed, for other Negroes can pick them out very easily. I have often thought about what would happen if all these Negroes were to reveal themselves. There would be some very upset white people all over the country.

The Navy decided to open a recreation center in the city of San Diego where sailors could go and buy beer cheaper than they could in town. They could take their female friends and dance to the music of one of the several Navy bands around San Diego. I had no idea what prompted the Navy to do this, for this recreational center (called Navy Field) was integrated.

It was the only place in San Diego that was, and from my point of view it had a lot of good points. Besides the cheap beer, Negroes in the Seaman-Fireman Branch could come into contact with the white firemen and seamen. We were interested in finding out whether we knew enough to do our jobs properly, and we made a point of talking to white sailors of the same classification. Motor machinists would talk to motor machinists, electricians to electricians, and so on. The white sailors were just as interested in us. I found out that I was not as dumb as I thought I was, especially concerning engines.

A sailor could take his female friend to Navy Field and not worry about any conflict with civilian men. Absolutely no civilian men were allowed into Navy Field, and none were allowed to hang around outside. This was a Navy recreation center for naval personnel and their guests only. If a civilian's wife or girlfriend was in Navy Field, that was just too bad; there were no civilian police in Navy Field.

A sailor didn't have to show any identification at Navy Field to buy beer, which was the only alcohol sold there. The issue of drinking age has been a pain in the ass to military personnel for a long time. The thought is that if someone takes an oath to give his life in the defense of his country, he should be able to buy a drink of whiskey or a beer if he chooses. The issue is complicated because military bases serve beer to their personnel without identification. When military personnel are in town, they are subject to arrest if they buy beer and are under the legal drinking age. It doesn't make much sense, does it?

By January 1944 my job was daily maintenance of all small boats used by the base. These whaleboats, liberty launches, cabin cruisers (leased to the Navy by civilians for a dollar a year), officers' boats, the commanding officer's boat (called the captain's gig), and picket boats all had various types of engines. My job was to check each one every morning to make sure that it was operational. I became the engineer on the captain's gig.

The captain's gig had been built here on the Frontier Base for the commanding officer. It was a twenty-eight-foot runabout with a hundred-octane V-8 Script engine. It had an oversized propeller and could do fifty miles an hour. It was governed down; it could go even faster. I didn't like this boat, for I had a fear of hundred-octane gasoline. It was sort of sweet-smelling and dangerous to use. It was the same gas used in airplanes.

The word got around the base that President Roosevelt had arrived at the U.S. Navy/Marine base in San Diego. We heard that the president was to stay on the Marine base overnight and go out sometime the next day.

Liberty for all crews of patrol boats was canceled, and every patrol boat that could go out was sent out with orders that nothing was to come within fifteen miles of the entrance to the San Diego harbor. My liberty was canceled automatically. I couldn't leave the base until the captain left, and at that time the captain had no intentions of going anywhere.

At about 9 P.M. the word came over the PA system for the engineer of the captain's gig to "man your boat," which meant that the captain was going out. I ran down to the boat and opened the covers over the motor. This was necessary to get the fumes from that hundred-octane gas out before I started the engine. For some unknown reason I had the idea that the damn motor would not start, but it did, and I waited for the captain. When he arrived, he had a submachine gun. We took off and crossed the antisubmarine net. The captain opened the throttle wide; the boat sat up upon its tail, and out into the night we sped. After a few miles we made a wide turn, came back to within a half-mile of the net, and throttled back to idle.

We were running very slowly toward the entrance to the harbor, and we could make out ships coming out of the harbor. There were five or six destroyers. Not far behind came the cruiser USS *Baltimore*. I felt proud that the president was on the ship named for my hometown. As the *Baltimore* approached we could see that she was tight; not the faintest light was showing. It was like looking down a gun barrel. As the *Baltimore* passed, the captain and I saluted. I was thinking that the president, on his return from wherever he was going, should have a talk with this captain who wasn't in harmony with his wishes, who openly practiced racism. The *Baltimore*, carrying President Roosevelt, passed into the night. I wrote the date and time on my locker door. Later I learned that the president had been on his way to meet Churchill and Stalin.

I had now been in the Navy a little over a year. I must say that my love for the Navy was growing each day, and my fascination with engines was increasing. It's hard to explain what causes a man to become fascinated by an engine. I believe it was the power produced by these engines that made me so interested in them. By this time I had achieved the rate of fireman first class.

In April 1944 I was called into the motor machinist office. The commander in charge of the motor machinist shop asked me if I wanted to attend the advanced service school for diesel in San Francisco. I could hardly answer. Attending an advanced service school had never entered my mind; the Navy was sending only its best men to these schools. The next day I boarded a train for the U.S. Navy's receiving station at San Francisco.

A receiving station is a place where naval personnel are sent for further transfer, either as individuals or as groups. The receiving station at San Francisco is located on Treasure Island, a man-made island almost in the middle of San Francisco Bay. Treasure Island is connected to San Francisco by a bridge that spans the bay, running from Oakland to San Francisco. The whole crew of a new ship had been assembled in this receiving station awaiting her commissioning.

Having presented my orders to the officer of the day at the receiving station, I was directed to a dorm in one of the large buildings on Treasure Island. With just a quick glance, I could tell that there were only Negroes in this dorm. Integration in the Navy had not gotten to the point that the races were going to be berthed together, at least not at any of the bases where I had been. I was also directed to watch the bulletin board for the draft that was going to the school. I was told that I would have to find a place to live in the city while I was going to the school, and that I would receive extra pay to cover my rent and food, because there was no place to berth the students at the school.

San Francisco was a lot different from any of the other cities I had visited. Although San Diego and San Francisco are in the same state, they differ greatly. Where San Diego had signs in windows and on doors stating "No Colored Allowed," there were no such signs in San Francisco, to my knowledge. Anywhere I chose to go in San Francisco I went with no embarrassment. As in every town or city I had been in, I found that the majority of the Negroes lived in one section of the city, around Fillmore and Webster Streets.

I had two work details while I was waiting for my draft. One was somewhat puzzling, and the other was disgusting. The puzzling detail was one where the guy in charge said that we would be finished in an hour. We did finish in that time frame; the reason we finished so quickly was that we were shoveling horse manure. Now, this seemed strange. I had yet to see a horse on Treasure Island, but they had to be there somewhere. This stuff didn't just grow in dark places; it was put there, and by horses. The other detail I was put on was the trash detail. This wasn't hard work; the detail merely rode around the base and dumped trash cans. The only problem was that Waves were on this base. I don't have too much to say about women in the military service except that the things these women put into trash cans were sickening, disgraceful, and it was plain disgusting that a man had to handle that type of trash. These women should have had incinerators in their dorms.

Still, I wasn't too upset about the details I was put on. I was engrossed in the fact that I would be going to service school and in all the possibilities that presented, such as the chance of a petty officer's rating. I daydreamed about the types of engines we were going to work on. I hoped that this could lead to the fulfillment of one of my dreams: to be an engineer on a PT boat.

On one of my trips into 'Frisco, on a rainy day, I went into a bar that I always frequented because I was never asked for ID there. It wasn't crowded; a couple of women were playing the jukebox. I went over to the door and stood watching the people out in the rain. One of the women playing the jukebox came over beside me and looked out.

She turned to me saying, "Guess what?"

"What?" I didn't have a clue what she was talking about, and wondered how long she had been there before I arrived.

"I don't have on anything except what you see."

I looked at her and said, "What are you telling me for? You want me to take you home and dress you?"

"That's possible," she said, smiling, and went back to the bar.

After a few seconds I went back to the bar and proceeded to find out just what she wanted to wear and when. That was the beginning of a relationship that lasted the rest of my time in San Francisco. She told me that she was married to a numbers backer who came home only twice a week, and she was tired of sitting at home. She said that she wanted to go out and have some fun. This woman took me all over 'Frisco. She bought me a navy trench coat with a big green dragon embroidered in the lining, and a watch. She paid for whatever we did.

After two weeks of checking the OGU (outgoing unit) bulletin board, I finally found a draft going to the International Harvester School for Advanced Diesel the next morning. Checking down the list I found "Newton, A. W., F1/C, 758-52-23." I was so happy that I couldn't keep still; I didn't sleep that night.

The next day I was ready to go hours before the time to assemble. When the time did arrive I took my sea bag over to the place outside the building and waited. Out came a master-at-arms. He began to call out the names of the men on the draft, and as he did, they got onto an open-body truck parked there. When he called my name, rate, and service number, I threw my sea bag onto the truck and climbed aboard.

"Just where do you think you're going?" the MA asked.

"You just called my name. I'm Newton. I'm going to the school."

"Get your bag and get off the truck. You're not going to this school."

"Why not? I'm on the draft. You just called my name. I was sent up here for this school. They sent me here from the Frontier Base."

"Coloreds don't go to this school. It's company policy. Get your bag and get off the truck. I'll have to check into this, but we can't hold these men up."

I was the only Negro in this draft, and as I picked up my bag I looked at the men around me. They were all looking at me, and only a couple of them had smiles on their faces. No one was talking, and I was very embarrassed. Tears were forming in the corners of my eyes. I fell back to the side and watched the rest of the men board the truck.

Just before the truck left I asked the MA, "Are you sure there's not some mistake?"

"There's no mistake. I'll find out what to do. Until then, just go to your dorm and wait until you hear from me."

The truck pulled off. Tears ran down my cheeks as I returned to my dorm. I threw my bag in a corner, fell onto an empty bunk, and cried. The Navy had sent me up here to attend this school, and I should have been allowed to go. I had thought the Navy knew who I was, and the policy now in the Navy was no discrimination. I couldn't understand why they would allow some company to tell them who could attend their schools. I cannot explain just how I felt; this rejection had hit me very hard.

After a few hours I returned to the OGU office and inquired about my going to the school, and I received the same answer: "We're checking on it."

I went into 'Frisco and told my girlfriend what had happened and she started crying. We both were sad, so we spent a sad evening together.

After two weeks of waiting, I gave up on going to the school. I was hanging around waiting for someone to make a decision as to what I was supposed to do next. I had been there so long that they made me MA over the dorm, which was good because I could go on liberty at one o'clock while the others awaiting transfers had to wait until four to go.

Up to this time I had never had much contact with the mess attendants or steward's mates in the Navy. Those I did come into contact with I never paid any attention to, since we were in different branches. But now that I had made MA in this dorm, I got to know everyone (all Negroes) who came into the dorm, to some degree. Talking to these mess attendants and steward's mates, I found out that whenever someone speaks of the "crew" of a Navy ship, he is not speaking of the mess attendants or steward's mates. They are not considered to be part of the crew and are classified as the lowest things in the Navy. They are berthed by themselves on board ship; on submarines, they are berthed in the torpedo rooms. Their general-quarters station (battle station) on ships is in the magazine. Now, the magazine is located in the bottom of the ship; if ever you go to Pearl Harbor and visit the *Arizona* memorial, just think of who didn't get out.

I asked about these things because I had heard so much about a Negro mess attendant, Dorie Miller, who shot down some Japanese planes during the attack on Pearl Harbor (the same person who had talked to us at Great Lakes). They said that this was true, that Miller had shot down some planes at Pearl Harbor, but he acted on his own. No mess attendant or steward's mate is trained to fire any guns on board any Navy ship, and that's why Dorie Miller received the high Navy decoration that he did get. I often wondered how he could have shot down those planes. I talked it over with other people many, many times. The only solution we could come up with was that prior to the attack on Pearl Harbor, the Navy had been lax, in a sense: it had somehow allowed somebody to show Dorie Miller how to operate a machine gun. And he must have been away from his general-quarters station during the attack; since the ship was in port and it was a Sunday morning, it stands to reason that he was not at his general-quarters station.

I met a steward who had just been transferred off a submarine. I spent the day talking to him, and he told me that he got off the sub the same day it left for Pearl Harbor. He was the captain's steward, and he told me that he had been at the home of his captain while the sub was in San Francisco. Later that day we went into San Francisco together. While we were sitting in one of the bars in the Fillmore District he asked me if I wanted to meet the captain's wife. I thought he was kidding, but he made a phone call. When he returned, he said that she would be there in about an hour. While we waited he told me about the affair he was having with this captain's wife.

A while later he said, "Here she comes." I turned toward the door, and a shapely white woman was coming toward us. He introduced me to her and ordered some drinks, and they began talking about the captain. He asked if the sub had left and if she had gone down to see the captain off, and so on. After a while I got into the conversation by asking her if she was really the wife of a sub captain; there was no reason to doubt what this steward was telling me, but I just asked. She reached into her purse and came out with a photo of a commander. His submarine pin was showing clearly.

I was thinking that if this commander knew of this, the Navy would be minus a steward, and if he came in while I was there the Navy might be minus a fireman, too. For some reason that girl in Tijuana came into my mind, and I was now convinced that white girls were too expensive. I bought the steward and the captain's wife a round of drinks and left. I guess the old saying "There are only two free persons in the United States: a white man and a Negro woman" is true. A white man can take a Negro woman anywhere he chooses and there is no comment, but as soon as a Negro man takes a white woman anywhere he is flirting with trouble.

I had the chance to meet a Negro second-class boatswain's mate who was passing through this receiving station. Upon our first meeting I got the impression that he was somewhat bitter. His stay was brief, but I did manage to talk to him over the course of a few days.

During one of our conversations he asked, "Have you ever been the only Negro on a ship, Newt?"

"No, why?" I couldn't figure out his reason for asking the question.

"If you ever find yourself in that situation, there's one thing you have to do. Find a white guy that's about your size, but one that you're pretty sure you can beat. Beat the hell out of him, really kick his ass. That's the only way you'll ever stop the white guys from picking on you. If you don't, the white sailors will push you around, and you'll never get any respect from them."

I laughed—probably because I couldn't think of anything to say.

"Go 'head on and laugh, but if you're ever in that situation, you'll find out what I'm talking about."

I had been in this receiving station for such a long time that I had forgotten exactly how long I had been there. My guess is that it had been around three months, and I had forgotten about attending any service school. They must have put my records somewhere and forgotten all about them.

One day in July I went to the OGU office and requested a ten-day leave to go home. They found my records, and the guy in the office asked me why I was still at Treasure Island. I told him if he didn't know why I was still at Treasure Island, then he shouldn't ask me because I really didn't know, either. I was soon on my way back to the Frontier Base in San Diego.

When I returned to the motor machinist shop, the division commander asked me how I had made out in school, and I told him I never reached the school and that Treasure Island was as far as I had been permitted to get, for they said it was company policy that no Negroes could attend that school. The division commander seemed to be somewhat embarrassed and instructed me to report to the shop for duty. I again requested a ten-day leave, and the division commander asked where I lived. He gave me a ten-day leave with six days' travel time and told me that I could leave the next day.

There was a slight problem, though. The round-trip fare from San Diego to Baltimore for a serviceman was around $90, and I had less than $50. I told a friend about my situation, and he advised me to go see the chaplain. He said that a lot of servicemen obtained loans for their fare home from the Red Cross. Since servicemen (firemen and seamen) made only around $50 to $60 a month, the Red Cross knew they had very little chance of getting home without help. They made loans for fares only to servicemen. These loans were to be paid back by monthly deductions from their pay.

I went to the chaplain and told him of my problem. He picked up the telephone, gave someone my name, rate, and serial number and the date I wanted to leave. After a few minutes he hung up and told me I could pick up my ticket at the train station the next day. I thanked him and left his office.

The next day I picked up my leave papers, went to the train station in San Diego, received my ticket from the Red Cross representative, and boarded the first of a series of trains to get home. I had to change trains in Chicago, where I had a four-hour layover.

Since I had some time to kill, I went over to the "El" to get a train to the South Park area. While I waited a girl came up. We looked at each other; for a long time we paid no attention to the trains going by. She walked over to a vendor to buy something. I went over and stood next to her.

She turned to me and said, "If I had a dime, I could call in sick, and I wouldn't have to go to work."

I gave her a dime, she called her job, and we caught a train to South Park. As soon as she opened the door to her apartment she started to take her clothes off, right inside the door. I said, "Hey, wait for me," and I also started to undress. In a few seconds there was a line of clothes stretching from the door to her bed.

After we came to our senses, I finally asked her name, which I immediately forgot. While I was getting dressed, she asked me to stay. I told her I had to catch a train but would be back the next week.

Upon arriving home, I learned that my best friend, Eddie, had joined the Navy and was at Great Lakes. Eight days at home wasn't enough time to do all the things I had planned. Before I knew it, it was time to leave, even though it seemed like I had just arrived.

My first priority when I reached Chicago was to get to Great Lakes and find Eddie. When I inquired about him there, I was told that he had been transferred to the naval hospital at Balboa Park in San Diego. Since I couldn't find Eddie, I tried to find the girl I had met on the way home. After a few unsuccessful attempts to get in touch with her, I caught a train for San Diego a day early.

A few nights later, while sitting in Navy Field, I saw Eddie coming my way. He hadn't seen me yet, so I lowered my head. As soon as he was beside me I said, "There goes that motherfucka. Let's get him." Eddie's head snapped around, and then he saw me. It was just like old times. We closed up Navy Field that night and the next.

I worked in the shop for about three weeks before I found my name on a draft of around forty men from the Frontier Base who were going to Shoemaker, California, which was the Navy's overseas training base. We formed outside the personnel office and boarded buses for the train station in San Diego. It was farewell to the Frontier Base. In the Navy when one is transferred it is said that all friendships and debts are canceled, so this was the end of a few debts and many friendships.

The station was loaded with Negro sailors bound for Shoemaker. We boarded the train. Our first stop was San Pedro, the center of California's fishing industry at that time, on the Los Angeles waterfront. The Navy had turned what looked like an old warehouse into a dorm. This was where we stayed until further orders, and we were to be "on our honor." That is, we were to be in the dorm from 7 A.M. to 4 P.M. with no one checking on us.

From San Pedro it was only a short ride to downtown Los Angeles. As always, the Negroes lived together in one area. It was no different here than in Virginia. The Negro came to California from the South in hopes of finding something called freedom. What he really found was segregation wrapped in a Christmas box. He still had segregation, but it looked prettier. The main street in Los Angeles for Negroes was Central Avenue. I gave up hope of ever seeing an orange tree in someone's yard.

Our orders finally came, and we again boarded a train for Shoemaker. This time we went all the way to the naval overseas training base. Here we were joined by another group, so now we formed a large group.

Shoemaker was a very large base near San Francisco. The mission of this base was to train naval personnel for combat. This combat training differed from what is normally taught to sailors; sailors generally learn warfare at sea, but here we learned land warfare. This training consisted of hand-to-hand combat, jungle warfare, and firing the new M1 carbine.

In combat in general, one rule supersedes all others: Kill or be killed. The officers impressed this on us every chance they got. In hand-to-hand combat, we found out, this could include some pretty gruesome acts. Our officers also stressed the fact that the reason the United States was having so many casualties in the war was that men were not doing what they were told. They emphasized that our chances of returning home would be much greater if we did things exactly as we were told.

Our training program at Shoemaker lasted about four weeks. Negro sailors and whites trained separately. We had liberty every weekend at Shoemaker.

One day we heard a rumor that we had better enjoy ourselves in San Francisco that weekend, because it would be our last. I decided that I had better not miss this one, so off to San Francisco I went. I had been in 'Frisco many times, and I had my favorite places to go. I called my friend and told her that I didn't think I would be seeing her for a while. Looking back, I should have waited until I was ready to return to camp to tell her. That was the worst weekend I had ever spent in 'Frisco. We went to several clubs, but the atmosphere was tense.

She waited until I was about to leave, and then she jumped all over me, wanting to know why I had to go and what I was fighting for. She said that Negroes had no business fighting in this war. She wanted me to desert, saying that I didn't have a flag to fight for.

I told her that I was born under this flag, and if I had to fight for any flag I would fight for this one, because this flag was the only one I knew. I also told her that things were beginning to break for the Negro in America, but it would take time and patience.

She was still against my leaving, even though I told her it was no use to try to stop me. As I was leaving, she came out into the hall and stood at the top of the steps calling me. I stopped and turned on the stairs as she was saying, "Don't go." I told her I would be back. As I closed the door, I looked back one last time. She was lying at the head of the steps, beating on the floor and hollering, "Don't go! Don't go!"

I closed the door and returned to Shoemaker.

The rumor about that being our last weekend turned out to be true. When we fell in for roll call that Monday morning, we were informed that we were leaving in one hour, but first we were going to be entertained by a USO show. We marched over to a hall where we listened to Count Basie's band. I will never forget the girl who sang "More Than You Know." I only wish I remembered her name.

We boarded buses and headed into San Francisco to the place of embarkation. This was a special area, surrounded by very high barbed-wire fencing. When one stepped off the bus, one was inside the fence. Once inside, no one could leave without proper authorization. There was no time wasted, and before I knew it, I was on board a ship. As I alighted on the deck of the ship I turned around, and to my surprise the upper deck of this pier was lined with people—white people! I didn't know any Negroes who knew when we were leaving, much less the pier number and the time. This sent a chill through me just thinking of all these people who knew the departure time of this troopship. The movement of troopships is generally kept very secret for reasons of security.

Because we had come on board in an all-Negro group, we were berthed in the same hold, or compartment. The other compartments were filled with whites. Everyone was excited, and we got back on deck as soon as possible after stowing our gear. I walked up and down the deck looking at all these people, and I didn't see one Negro on that pier. I didn't have much time to reflect on that because they were lowering the gangway and dropping the lines. Soon, amid all the confusion of farewells, the ship moved away from the dock, slowly down the bay toward the Golden Gate. Everyone became quiet. I noticed that tears were falling all over the place as we moved under the Golden Gate Bridge.

5 *Sailor*

The tears didn't last long; they soon turned into sea-
sickness. The water around San Francisco Bay is the
roughest water one can find outside of any harbor.
But we soon got over that and were on our way without an escort. We were making this trip alone. Now
I really had thoughts about those people back on the
pier. If one of those people was a spy, we were going
to be SOL. On the third day out, we were informed
that our destination was Milne Bay, New Guinea. I
had an idea where New Guinea was but didn't have a
clue about Milne Bay.

During the day we would gather topside around
the holds we had been assigned to, either on deck or
on the hatch. There is absolutely nothing to do on
board a troopship, so we sharpened our dirks, the
knives that had been issued to us. These dirks were so
sharp, we could shave with them. Whenever we were
in rough water, the menu was sandwiches. I think this
was partly because the cooks had to prepare something quick, but also maybe because no one was going

to eat a lot under those conditions. You ate and slept and lay on the deck and talked and thought. You did more thinking than anything else.

I would think about home and some of the things that my father had told me about, like when he was fourteen years old and took to the sea. He used to say if you ever do anything wrong, don't cry when you get hurt. As a little boy I would sit around and listen to him as he talked to his friends on the subject of the Negro. Father would say that in order for the Negro to make his move for equal rights, two things must happen. First, the older generation of Negroes (that is, the Negroes of his parents' age) must die off, because they wouldn't allow their children or grandchildren to buck the white man's system (during this time older Negroes had a strong influence over their children and grandchildren). Second, the Negro must have a black leader. We had some leaders, but they were light-skinned, and the black Negro would not follow them. This black leader must be a man of intelligence and must not be afraid to lead his people in their quest for equality. The thing that hurt the most about this was the fact that there were no prospects for strong leaders in view, so the Negro had to wait and wait and wait. My father's friends all agreed with him on this subject.

Some of the things my father used to say made me laugh even though the situation wasn't funny. For instance, whenever he or someone else was in a very difficult situation he would say, "There is honey in horse manure, but it takes a bee to get it out." I always thought that was one of those sayings that would mean something to me as I got older, but now I'm not sure I'll ever be old enough to figure that one out.

Two weeks out of San Francisco an announcement came over the PA system: "You polliwogs, you scum of the earth, your day is coming." Every night until we crossed the equator there was some kind of threat. We found out that this was part of the Shellback Initiation, a ritual that occurred whenever a Navy ship crossed the equator. Anyone who has not crossed the equator is a polliwog; anyone who has is a shellback. As the crossing is made, polliwogs become members of Neptune's Order of the Deep: shellbacks.

On the day we crossed, there was a massive initiation. We polliwogs were told to wear only our shorts. We were blindfolded and led out of the hold onto the deck. We were painted with some kind of dye. They put cold spaghetti in our mouths and told us we were eating worms; guys were throwing up all over the place. Then they pointed us in a direction and told us when we reached the bulkhead (wall) we would be shellbacks. They didn't tell us that there were about fifteen guys with fire hoses between us and that bulkhead. It was really an experience, being blindfolded and trying to get to that bulkhead through all that water.

The old myth about no smoking on deck after dark was soon put to rest. There was an announcement that we could smoke on deck after dark, though we were not to strike any matches. The ship ran a zigzag course during the day and a straight course at night. I later found that these were all basic security measures, designed to make it a little harder for the enemy to find us or figure out what we were doing. These things helped to remind me that there was a war going on.

There was not enough fresh water on board ship to allow us to take showers. One could take a saltwater shower, but regular soap wouldn't dissolve in salt water. We had something called "saltwater soap," but that wouldn't dissolve in salt water, either. The only alternative was to wait until it rained to take a shower. We had only two rains on the trip. After twenty-three days aboard that ship, we were glad to get to New Guinea; we would have been glad to get anyplace.

Looking at New Guinea from the sea, we saw a very beautiful deep green. As far as we could see, this beauty was unbroken, except along the shore where the various military installations were built; the Navy had a receiving station and some other facilities there. We didn't see any of the Japanese, wild boar, black widow spiders, natives, or snakes that we had been warned about; New Guinea has the biggest snakes in the world.

Disembarking into a large open area, we were addressed by a seaman with a forty-five strapped to his side. His welcome speech was short and not very sweet.

"Attention, men. Welcome to Gammadodo, Milne Bay, New Guinea. Gammadodo is just your point of disembarkation; your stay here will be as brief as possible. The first thing you need to know is that all of you have left your ratings on that ship. While you are here, you all have the same rating, and you will all be treated the same. You are not to leave the confines of this base for any reason. There are still Japs around, and the natives are not extremely friendly; in fact, they are headhunters." This might have been just a scare tactic, but it was enough for me.

The seaman then called out names and assigned us to dorms. The dorms were two-story buildings, much longer than they were wide, and they had no sides. There was only a railing running around them, top and bottom. It was the first time I had ever seen a building like that. It was also my first time to sleep on a cot, and my first time to sleep under a mosquito net. We had been warned about the mosquitoes here, which we called dive bombers. I got bitten on the lip by one, and my lip swelled to twice its normal size. You soon learned that your best friends were a mosquito net and a can of insect spray. In the tropics mosquitoes carry a disease called malaria that could render an army defenseless overnight. To combat this we had been given Atabrine tablets since the second day out of 'Frisco. We took these tablets three times a day, at mealtime, or we didn't eat. We continued to take them as long as we were in the tropics. This Atabrine has a side effect: after a while everyone will have a yellowish tinge to his skin. Otherwise, it is invaluable.

We only had cold showers. A cold shower may seem pleasant to some, but to me it is a gruesome thing. As long as I was in the tropics I never went into a shower willingly, although I did go daily.

After three days I was on draft with about thirty other Negroes who had been on the same ship. Our destination was a repair base across the bay, known as LCMU 26 (Landing Craft Maintenance Unit 26). We were met on the dock by a chief petty officer. We stacked our gear, went to the mess hall for chow, and came back to the dock. We then boarded a truck and were taken about two miles down the road to a group of huts that appeared to have been abandoned for some time.

These huts were built on stilts about seven feet off the ground. All we had was a roof, a table, and some chairs. There were no sides on those huts—just a railing; it was warm all the time, and you needed all the air you could get. There was a basketball court in front of the huts, and about thirty feet behind them was the edge of the jungle. The chief instructed us to clean up the huts and move in. On the truck were brooms, cots, mosquito nets, mattresses, and kerosene lamps. We cleaned up the huts and set up our cots and nets. The truck returned and took us up to the base for chow and then back to the huts.

The first night in the huts, everyone slept with one eye open. We knew that there were dangerous things out there in the jungle. That didn't worry us; what we were concerned about was whether any of these things could be inside the huts with us. Someone threw a shoe. The lights came on in every hut and stayed on all night.

The next day the truck came to take us to the base. This was the first time we were to eat with the white personnel. The first question that came into our minds was, Where do these people sleep? Certainly they were not down two miles away on the edge of the jungle where we were. We later found out that the white personnel were quartered in Quonset huts not far from the mess hall on the base property. The whites sat at tables that were all white, and we sat at tables that were all Negro. We stared at one another throughout the meal.

After chow we were taken to the shop, which was designed for overhaul work. The chief assigned us jobs: two men at each of the ten overhaul stands, one in the tool crib, one in the parts storeroom, and two to haul the engines between the boats and the shop. I was a fireman first class in charge of one of the overhaul stands. We had twenty-four working hours to overhaul an engine, working eight-hour days. Every three days an engine must be completed and ready to test. A civilian employed by General Motors, who had no authority over us, was in charge of the testing stand. His job was to test these engines, which were used in most of the Navy's landing craft. These boats were then loaded onto ships to be transported north. Rumor had it that they were to be used to invade the Philippines.

That first night we had a meeting in reference to the mess hall. It was our feeling that the segregated seating could not continue. It was an insult and exactly the kind of situation we felt that our presence in the Navy was supposed to eliminate. There was no one to complain to, though. As they had told us at Great Lakes, there were no guidelines to follow; we would have to use our heads. So we came up with a plan. We would stop going to the mess hall in groups, and we would sit so that there was a maximum of three Negroes at a table. We figured that in the beginning the white personnel would move to other tables, creating the same segregated situation as before, but eventually they would get tired of moving every time a Negro sat beside them. We knew that these white guys had never sat at the same table with Negroes before, but they would have to get used to it.

The plan worked, although I don't remember a white sailor on the base ever holding a conversation with a Negro. In fact, the only white personnel I ever spoke with were the commander, the chief petty officer in charge of the shop, and the civilian who tested the engines. But we were satisfied that we had the white sailors sitting at the same table with us. Other things would come later, we hoped.

We had been warned not to venture into the jungle because of the natives around the base. If we found ourselves outside the base, we were not to make any advances toward the native women, for the native men would kill us. We were told that these natives would kill someone just for sport.

I had, on occasion, come to within three or four feet of these native men. Believe me, they were not to be fooled with. Their hair grew straight out. They colored their hair; some had green hair, others blond, black, or red. They chewed a berry that is found in the jungle called a betel nut. Betel nuts also came in colors, so their teeth were red, black, green, and yellow. Their skin color was a deep brown—not black, but not far from it. A sickening thing about their appearance was that their skin peeled, so they weren't something you would like to look at or have coming after you. They spoke no English, and I didn't know what language they were speaking, so we just stared at each other whenever we met. Maybe I looked as strange to them as they looked to me. The only thing I knew to do in a situation like that was to move out smartly.

The women looked like the men, except that their hair was longer, and the older women's breasts hung down to their navels. They wore skirts made of some type of grass. The strips of grass were about a quarter inch wide and two feet long. The skirt went three-quarters of the way around the waist, but each woman wore about ten of them. It was a tossup who was more fierce, the native men or the native women. I believed that the men were afraid of the women, and I didn't want anything to do with either one of them.

Three days a week we went to a beer hall, where we were given two cans of beer. Those who didn't drink beer were given three Cokes. The first time we entered this place we encountered the same snub as in the mess hall. This didn't last long, though, because the fellows in the beer hall were thinking about home. Someone played a record by the Mills Brothers, "Till Then," and almost every man in the hall cried. Each time we went to the beer hall, these guys would cry when that record was played. Sometimes it was played four or five times. What made this song hurt so much was the fact that no one knew if there was going to be a "then."

The lack of available women had an effect on the men. One funny thing about women is that you really don't have any idea how much you would miss them until you are in a place like this where they are scarce. Word came to us that there were some Negro women Red Cross workers at an Army camp about five miles up the road. Some of us piled into a truck and went to check them out. True, there were three Negro women Red Cross workers there, passing out coffee and doughnuts to the Negro soldiers. There was also an armed guard behind each one. At the time I couldn't understand why they needed guards, but it was a treat just to hear their voices. We drank our coffee, ate our doughnuts, and just looked at them for a while. We left happy that we had at least had a look at an American woman and had exchanged a few words with her.

As I said, there was a basketball court in front of our huts, alongside the main road. In the evenings we would play, mostly to tire ourselves out so that we could sleep. Afterward we would shower and sit around the huts in our shorts until we felt like going to bed. Taps wasn't played overseas, in the war zone, so it was up to us when we went to sleep. One of the guys started appearing on the basketball court in a pair of women's underwear he found in the bales of rags that we used in the shop. This attracted the attention of the few white nurses who drove past. They would stop and look and laugh. This prompted the rest of us to search for women's underwear. Soon we all were playing in women's underwear. Sometimes there would be four or five jeeps with nurses and officers parked along the road watching us play. They got a kick out of seeing men in women's underwear, and we got a kick out of looking at them, especially the nurses. Now we didn't have to go find women to look at; they were coming to see us. We played every day that it didn't rain.

When it rained in the jungle over there, it rained not for hours but for days—sometimes a week. We had been accustomed to staying inside when it rained, but after being there for a while you can forget that it's raining. We sat for hours in an open theater in the rain and thought nothing of it. One reason was that although it was raining, it was still hot. The foul-weather gear that the Navy gave us was no protection because it was hot and quickly became waterlogged. It was better not to use it; we were going to get wet anyway in the constant downpour. We were lucky; we didn't have to work in the rain like some of the other guys.

Everything was proceeding well in the shop. We were overhauling the engines according to the book, and they were being checked by the manufacturer's representative. Sometimes when we had a few spare minutes I would go watch the chief overhaul the injectors, blowers, and pumps. He asked if I was interested in learning to overhaul these parts. After I told him I was, he showed me the techniques. Soon I was taken off the overhaul stand and placed in charge of the injector, blower, and pump rooms. I decided which parts would or would not be replaced. These critical decisions were based on accurate use of feeler gauges and close visual inspection. An irregularity of a few thousandths of an inch or a little salt deposit would cause these parts to malfunction. This was a pretty important responsibility, one that I wouldn't have had if it hadn't been for the chief.

One other incident happened that showed me how fair the chief was. One day one of the fellows on the overhaul stand came into the blower room and told me that the captain was in the shop. I hadn't seen the commanding officer of the base prior to this. I went to the door and looked. To my surprise, he was only a lieutenant, but he was called the captain because of the position he held. Someone came in and requested a blower so that he could test an engine that had just been overhauled. This was the final step before turning the engine over to the manufacturer's rep.

We started the engine without the air silencer (air filter) connected to the blower, which was against the book, but it was the way things were done in that shop. Whenever one of those engines was started without the air silencer, a clattering sound would come from the open blower intake port. The captain heard the clattering and thought that something was wrong.

"Chief, there's a problem with this engine. What's that godawful noise?"

The chief came over. "Sir, that's perfectly natural. The engine's fine."

"I've never heard a noise like that from an engine. There's something wrong."

"Sir, the noise is coming from the intake port on the blower. In normal operation it's covered by the air silencer. Since there's no silencer on the engine, you have air rushing through, and that's what makes that noise."

By this time the manufacturer's rep had come over, and he nodded in agreement. "That's exactly right, sir, the engine's working exactly the way it's designed."

The captain completely ignored the civilian and turned to face the chief. "I want you to take this blower off and personally inspect it. Is that understood?"

"Newton, take the blower off." The chief turned to me with a look of resignation.

I removed the blower and took it back to the blower room. The captain followed and stood looking right over my shoulder while I removed the cover plates and gears, so that the chief could check the blower out with his feeler gauges. The chief laid out the manual with the specifications and carefully checked all the clearances.

When he finished, he turned to the captain. "Sir, this blower checks out perfectly. This man knows what he's doing."

Determined to exercise his authority, the captain said, "I want a new blower put on that engine."

The chief nodded to me. "Newton, let's get a new blower on the engine."

I got a new blower out of the parts storeroom and connected it to the engine. When the civilian started the engine, the blower emitted the same noise.

"That's much better; that's more like it," the captain said. He left the shop.

The chief gave me a knowing look and shook his head. "Newton, put that blower on the next engine to be tested." I had the feeling that he was even more fed up with the captain than I was.

One day in the injector room I turned to find one of the natives standing behind me holding a pineapple. Since we couldn't understand each other, I had no idea what he wanted to trade it for. Pineapples grew wild over there, so they weren't worth anything. He picked up a flashlight that was lying on the bench. I shook my head "No" and reached for the flashlight, but he drew away and held out the pineapple. I again shook my head, and he still held the pineapple out to me. Then I noticed that he had a gleaming machete at his side, and I decided that the man had made a reasonable offer after all and that I was in no mood to argue. Anyhow, the Navy had plenty of flashlights. I kept the door to the room locked after that in case he came back for batteries.

Every now and then we would gather in one of the huts to discuss what we were going to do about various situations. We believed that this command was biased. For example, there was no reason for us to be stuck out in the jungle in those huts; we knew there was room for us on the base because the white boys we had replaced had been housed there. But as before, there was no one we could go to with our complaints.

So we stayed in the huts and tried to make the best of it. Sometimes we played jokes on one another. For example, someone would tie a black thread to another guy's mosquito net and pull on the thread when the lights went out. When the net moved, the guy was definitely going to come out of that bed. But out there in the jungle was really no place to play jokes; they could get you killed. One time a guy killed a big snake outside the hut. Someone got the idea of leaving the snake coiled up in the bed of the sailor who was on watch. When he came in and lifted his mosquito net and saw that snake, he screamed. We all laughed until he reached under his mattress, pulled out his carbine, and ordered everyone out of bed. He was mad, but thankfully he soon cooled off.

One day five other guys in the shop and I were placed on transfer to the receiving station across the bay. Gammadodo did not excite me my second time around. There was a big draft there awaiting orders to move out. This draft occupied two dorms, which meant that it was hundreds of men. I was thinking that I would like to go with this draft, even though nobody knew where it was going. Nobody cared where it was going; not knowing was what made it so exciting. Aside from that, some of the guys on this draft had come over with me from the States.

I soon learned that there was a lot of dissension among the Negro men in the base company on Gammadodo. They were hopping mad about the Navy placing white petty officers over them and not allowing Negroes to be promoted to these positions, even though the Negroes were qualified and experienced. They said that they were tired of this stuff and were going to do something about it. They claimed to have enough guns and ammunition hidden away to get what they wanted. They were so frustrated, they were past the stage of taking advice. I sympathized with them. There was no doubt that a riot was in the making, though the Navy could avert it simply by letting the Negroes take the tests for the positions in question.

I told one of the leaders of this group that if he had so many weapons hidden away, I would like a carbine. That night as I lay in my cot, a fellow came up, shoved a carbine with a full magazine under the cot, and left without a word. There was only one place I could carry this gun, and that was in my sea bag. I broke the gun down just as we had been trained at Shoemaker, placed it in the middle of my sea bag, and packed clothes around it. I didn't know what I was going to do with it, but I felt better having it.

The routine at this receiving station was the same as at any other. You got up and sat around till they posted the drafts. If you weren't on the draft, you went back to your rack and slept. One evening after chow I decided to take a walk around the base and see what was going on. I was amazed by the size of the place. It was much larger than I had thought. It was beginning to get dark, and I was heading back to my dorm when a friend ran up.

"Hey, Newton! I've been looking all over the base for you. Come on, man, we're on draft."

I said, "I checked the draft this morning and didn't see our names on it."

"It wasn't posted in our dorm, but it was in the dorm of the big draft waiting to go out. We'd better hurry; they're loading now."

We ran to our dorm, picked up our sea bags, and hurried down to the dock. There were a couple of ships tied up there; one was illuminated by floodlights from the dock. She was painted white from her stack to the waterline. This seemed odd. All the ships I had seen since the war started were painted either camouflage or dull gray; I had never seen a white ship.

I went to the gangway. The officer there asked, "What is your name, rate, and serial number?"

"Newton, A.W., Fireman First Class, 758-52-23," I answered.

He checked the list. I doubted that I was on this draft as my friend had said, but I knew I would soon find out.

The officer said, "Adolph W. Newton."

I said, "Yes, sir."

"You are to bunk in #2 hold and muster with NABU 6."

"Yes, sir," I answered, and went aboard that gleaming white ship, followed by my friend. About an hour later the ship eased out into the night. I didn't know where we were going, but I knew we weren't going home.

The next day we were informed over the PA system that we were on board the Dutchmaster *Sommelsdyke,* and we were to rendezvous with a convoy at Hollandia, New Guinea. Hollandia was the headquarters of the commanding officer of the Seventh Fleet, Admiral Kinkaid. The code name for his headquarters was Anchor Section. Hollandia was a spectacle to behold. As far as one could see, there were ships. I have never seen or heard of such a gathering of ships of so many different nations. Two days later this great convoy was on the move heading north.

This group that I mustered with was known as NABU (Naval Advance Base Unit) 6. All of the personnel needed for a complete supply base were on this ship. In the holds of the ship was all the equipment needed on the base. Each group was a specific part of the function of the base: medical, administration, motor pool, cooks and bakers, and a base company. Each group was given a name: NABU 1, 2, 3, and so on. My group, NABU 6, was the motor pool.

The routine on board ship was the same as on any troopship, except that we had a lot more room. This ship was carrying only the personnel for this supply base. I encountered no incidents of racial discrimination. In fact the white fellows seemed to welcome me, so I was at ease.

I had a lot of time to think about that repair base in New Guinea. The way the Negroes were treated there kept going through my mind. I made up my mind that since there was nothing to guide this experiment at integration, I would have to make my own rules. The only thing to guide me was Right. I was going to go where these white sailors went, do whatever they did, eat where they ate, sleep where they slept. I had to project myself among these men and let Right be my guide. I could not let another situation develop like the one we had endured at the repair base in New Guinea. It was my firm intention to seek equal treatment, and I would demand this regardless of the consequences. I was going to use my head, for I didn't want to get into something I didn't understand or something I couldn't see through to completion. It had to be done right, even if it was hard.

Each day we had air-raid drills, and each day we were told that we had to get down into the holds faster. We got to the point that we could clear the deck in thirty seconds.

I was lying on the deck one day and began to laugh.

One of the guys asked, "What in the hell is funny?"

I said, "I was thinking of a joke my father's been telling for years. I never saw anything funny about it, but my father and his friends would crack up laughing at it."

"Tell it; let me see if I get it."

"It goes like this. One day a guy named Hanna was on his knees praying, and he was telling the Lord, 'Lord, my people need a leader down here, and Lord, this is Hanna speaking.'"

My friend didn't laugh; I don't guess he got it.

We arrived at Leyte, Philippine Islands. From the sea this land did not appear to be as beautiful as New Guinea, but that made no difference to us—just as long as it was land.

The air raids that we had in Leyte Gulf were no drills. The Japanese put air strikes into this area at least four times a day. That meant that we hurried into the holds of the ship four times a day without incident.

The spot where we were anchored was opposite the Seventh Fleet headquarters on Leyte. The town or village was called Tolosa. We could see the island of Samar on one side and Leyte on the other. It was said that the two came so close together that one could walk from one island to the other.

Word came over the PA system that we were going to set up our base on Samar, which was forty miles away. We weighed anchor and headed southeast, dropping anchor three miles off the shore of Samar. This area was full of ships being unloaded. We still had those daily air raids by the Japanese.

It was announced over the PA system that we were to disembark the next day, which happened to be Christmas Day, 1944. We stacked all our sea bags on the stern of the ship. The booms were rigged, and all was ready for our early-morning disembarkation. We were excited about going ashore. Several LCMs (landing craft, mechanized) came from the shore to help.

"Now hear this!" came over the PA system.

Another voice said, "This is the captain. Since tomorrow is Christmas Day, it is my decision to stay aboard for Christmas in order that we all can have Christmas dinner, which we can't do if we disembark. I have been informed that the galley could not be set up in time to serve a Christmas dinner. I want to wish you all a Merry Christmas."

That night as I lay down on the deck, my thoughts began to drift back to the Christmas Eves I'd had at home. We children used to hang our stockings on the mantel and go to bed to await the coming of Santa Claus. I really had believed that there was a Santa Claus, but that was five years ago, when I was a child of fourteen. For some reason I was wishing that I could be that child again. Instead, I was now a man of nineteen and in some place I had never heard of, thousands of miles from home with only memories to console me as I lay upon the hatch. I looked up into the sky, picked out a big, bright star, let my mind hang my stocking on that star, put out that bright light, and went to sleep.

Christmas Day was nothing like those I remembered. We ate our breakfast and lunch and then had a very nice Christmas dinner with (almost) all the trimmings. The mailman had been ashore and returned with some new recordings. The two songs that were played most that day were Ella Fitzgerald's "Into Each Life Some Rain Must Fall" and the Ink Spots' "Making Believe."

That evening my friend Joe and I were lying on the deck talking about the captain. I asked, "Why does the captain have an armed escort whenever he comes on deck?"

Joe said, "That's his protection in case somebody wants to take a poke at him."

I asked, "Who would want to lower the boom on the captain? And for what reason?"

Joe said, "That is the reason: they don't know who."

The word came over the PA to change the watch. It was eight o'clock, Christmas night. The moon was shining brightly. Joe said, "There goes that song, 'Making Believe,' again."

I said, "Yeah, that's about the umpteenth time they've played it since the mailman brought it on board this morning."

Suddenly we both sat up. There was a noise that we couldn't identify; it was a "whoooing" sound. We couldn't tell what it was or from which direction it was coming, and it was getting louder.

Someone yelled out, "We're being shelled by a submarine!"

All hell broke out on the deck. There was total confusion and panic. There was but one thought in everyone's mind: to get below deck. We had practiced this drill, time and time again. We could clear the deck in thirty seconds. During the daily raids by Japanese aircraft, we were almost flawless in this drill, but not this night.

Joe and I ran to the hatch leading to our hold (#2 hold) only to find it so jammed that men were stuck in the opening, and no one could go down the ladder. We ran around to the hatch leading to #1 hold, only to find that it too was jammed, men hollering and pushing in an effort to get below. We then hid beside a winch.

After a moment Joe said, "I'm going back around to #1."

I went back to #2, but the situation was the same as before. My heart was pounding so hard that I thought my chest was going to burst. Fear and panic had complete control of us all. I dove into a gutter alongside the hatch. I was facing forward. As soon as I was in the gutter there was a big explosion. BEEDOOM! Yellow and red flames shot up out of #1 hold.

I buried my face in my hands and said, "Oh, Mother! Oh, Mother! What have I gotten myself into?"

Someone was running down the deck when the explosion occurred. He was thrown head over heels onto the deck and dropped a life jacket. Self-preservation took hold of me; I rolled across the deck, grabbed the life jacket, and ran toward the stern of the ship, away from the fire. As I ran down the deck, I saw that most of the booms that were rigged for unloading the next day had fallen, and there were men lying all over the deck. They were calling out the names of women and "Oh, Mother!" and "Oh, Father!"

I didn't stop—I couldn't stop, for panic had gripped me, and my only thought was to get to the stern of the ship, away from the fire. To my surprise, the men on the stern didn't know that anything was wrong. They thought the gun crew was practicing. I started to laugh. I have no idea what made me do that, for I was still scared.

One of the fellows asked, "What are you laughing at?"

I said nothing for a moment. Then I answered, "We've been hit, and the ship is sinking." Now the alarms were going off, and the signalman was on the signal light. This light was red. It was the first time I had ever seen a red signal light, but I knew very well what it meant. Men were coming out of the holds now, wanting to know what was going on. It was then that I learned what had happened. It seemed like a year had gone by since we first heard that sound, but it had only been about a minute.

One of the fellows who saw what had happened said that a Japanese plane had stolen in on us with his engines cut off. The noise that we heard was the propellers turning in the air. It was one of those suicide planes, because after he put that torpedo into our port bow he tried to bank into our midships, but his wing tip touched the water, and he flipped over into the sea.

We had cut our anchor chain and were under way toward the shore. A destroyer came alongside and used her bullhorn to inform the bridge of the condition of our ship. It was not good. We all gathered on the starboard side of the ship where the destroyer was. The person using the bullhorn told us not to group on one side of the ship because she might capsize, so we spread out.

Joe came up to me. "Hey, Newton!"

"I thought that you went down into #1 hold."

"I did, but I came out when we got hit. If you wet your shirt, you can go to sick bay and tell them it's acid. You'll get a Purple Heart. That's what I did; I'm gonna get mine."

I didn't go to sick bay; I was worried that the ship was going to sink.

Word came over the PA system: "This is the captain. Prepare to abandon ship."

I went to the side of the ship and looked to see if any boats were alongside. There were several boats below.

Word came over the PA system: "This is the captain. Abandon ship!"

Over the side I went. There were cargo nets in place, which we were to have used the next day to disembark. When the boat pulled away from the ship, I was up on the ramp of an LCM. I lit a cigarette and said to myself, *You didn't get me that time, you SOB.*

We went around to the port side of the ship. We could see the big hole that the torpedo had put in the old lady. They said it was thirty feet wide. Then everyone got quiet, for we all knew that there had been men in #1 hold where she got hit. The fact that #1 had been too jammed for more of us to get down there surely saved some lives. We stared at that now very pink fire coming out of that hole in her side and out of the #1 hatch. We could see the propellers turning as the old lady tried to run aground in shallow water. She was sinking.

We had to go quite a distance from the ship to shore. While we watched the ship burn, I relived the hellish moments of the attack. One thing I kept going over and over in my mind was that when I was running down the deck and those men were calling out the names of women, I couldn't recall anyone calling out to the Lord. This I couldn't understand, being from a very religious family. I then recalled that I hadn't called upon the Lord, either. One thing was for certain: I wasn't the same person who had boarded that ship in New Guinea.

When we reached the shore, we all scrambled out of the LCM and were relieved to be on land again. The men on the shore were wondering where all these men were coming from. One came up to me. "Where are all you guys coming from?"

I pointed to the faint red light far out in the bay and said, "That's our ship, and we were just hit by a torpedo."

He said, "Oh, yeah," and walked away.

I couldn't understand that "don't give a damn attitude" of his, but I put him out of my mind and watched the faint red glow out in the bay. It seemed to be standing still, but I knew it was moving very slowly toward the shore.

We were told to form in front of the church in the town. This church was the largest structure in town. It was made of stone while the houses were made of bamboo. This was a Catholic church and the only one in the town. The officers tried to hold a roll call there in the dark, using a flashlight to read, but so many fellows were missing that they decided to wait till morning. We were told to stay near the church. We stretched out on the ground, and that's where we slept that Christmas night.

6 *Overseas War*

The next day we were told that there was not one camp on the island, either Army or Navy, that could feed all of us. We were split up into groups and taken to the various camps within a mile to eat breakfast. My group was taken to an Army Engineers camp, which was all Negro. As I looked at my group, I noticed that we were all Negro, too.

We didn't have any mess kits because all of our equipment had been lost when the ship was torpedoed. Someone at the camp came up with some extra mess kits—not enough for all of us, but it was all they had. The kits came in two parts, so we each got half a kit and a spoon. The Army guys told us to hang on to these; if we wanted to eat again, half a kit would have to do. I don't know just what we ate that day, but it was food, and we were still nervous from that torpedo.

On the way back to the church, we had an air raid, and we scattered into the jungle; we were convinced as to the damage an airplane could do. I wasn't as afraid as I had been the night before, though; I was certain that nothing could ever frighten me that badly again. The all-clear sounded, and we returned to the church. There we heard that a boat crew had picked up the Jap pilot who had torpedoed us last night, and they were bringing him in. We all went down to the dock to get a look at him.

An LCM came into the dock and tied up. The body of a Japanese pilot was lying on the deck behind the cockpit. His hands were tied behind his back; his legs were tied at the ankles. There were three bullet holes in his face. The fact that he was bound hand and foot led me to believe that he had been alive when they pulled him from the bay. The way the guys on the boat were smiling only strengthened my belief. The Navy hymn ran through my mind:

> *Eternal Father, strong to save,*
> *Whose arm hath bound the restless wave,*
> *Who bidd'st the mighty ocean deep*
> *Its own appointed limits keep,*
> *O hear us when we cry to thee*
> *For those in peril on the sea!*

The body was put on a weapons carrier. The white fellows started to curse him, then someone pulled out a dirk and plunged the blade into the lifeless body; then more people began to stab the body.

The killing of the Jap pilot didn't disturb me, for only the night before he had killed some of my shipmates, but I was bothered by the way they treated his body. Not only did they stab it repeatedly, but someone pulled the teeth from the body, and they called him awful names. I stood there and watched and wondered if they would do that to me. From somewhere came the answer: Yes! It all reminded me of some of the pictures I had seen of the lynching of Negroes in the southern part of the United States.

An officer called us together at the church. "Men, I want you to know that we are up that famous creek, and we don't have a paddle. The word is that we have lost most of the equipment on our ship. We'll salvage what we can over the next couple of days. We've asked around the island. There are no extra tents that we can get, there are no extra cots, and we hope by tomorrow to be able to feed you in a group. In the meantime, we have permission for you to sleep in this church. You are to eat at the same places you ate this morning, after which you are to stay close by the church. That is all."

The next day it started to rain, and we stayed inside the church most of the time. That night an officer ordered us back out into the rain. We were informed that someone had taken a crap in the church, and the priest had requested that we leave, no questions asked.

The next day we were called together in the rain. The officer said, "We have now received an ample number of tents, but there is still one more problem. The area we have selected to pitch these tents is that walled-in graveyard."

We looked at one another stupidly, then we looked at that walled-in graveyard with all its headstones and markers. I was thinking that I had slept in some of the damnedest places, but this would top them all.

The officer continued, "Let's turn to and clear that area of those head-stones and markers and get these tents erected."

It didn't take long to get the tents set up; we realized that this was going to be our only shelter for a while. The tents could hold six or eight men. Each had room for a table in the middle. We didn't have any light, so when it got dark we went in. That night we slept inside the tents, but we had no cots or blankets. We were soaked to the skin, but this didn't bother us as we stretched out and slept on the muddy ground. At least we were inside and out of the rain.

The next day we received enough cots for each man to have one. We were now eating at a U.S. Navy construction battalion (Seabee) base across the road. Because we had lost all of our equipment, the plan to set up a supply base was canceled. At night some of us used to go over to the Seabee base to hear a very interesting radio program that came on then. It was the most famous radio program in the Pacific theater of war. The girl on the program was "Tokyo Rose," and she broadcast Japanese propaganda. One night she promised this particular Seabee outfit "a visit by some friends from the air." The rains had stopped, and we spent another night without sleep, but nothing happened. I wondered where Tokyo Rose was getting her recordings, because she seemed to have better and more up-to-date records than the American radio program "GI Jill."

One day Joe and I hopped a ride out to our ship. The old girl had made it to a reef, where her bow had settled down with her propellers clear of the water. We went aboard as far as #1 hold and looked in. There was no ladder leading down into the hold.

I said to Joe, "I thought you said that you were down in #1 hold when that torpedo hit."

He said, "I was, and I came back up the ladder."

I still don't know how he did it, but strange things happen in war.

A work party was eventually sent out to the ship. They recovered the gear we had stacked on deck the day before the ship was hit. We now had a change of clothes and a cot with a mattress and netting. We called this place the Receiving Station in the Graveyard on Samar.

About a week later Joe, two other Negroes named Al and Nap, and I were on draft to the Anchor Section (Seventh Fleet headquarters) on Leyte. The LCI (landing craft, infantry) that carried us over to Leyte came to a stop on the beach in front of a village called Tolosa, which was a beehive of activity. There were two high-ranking officers for every enlisted man there.

One thing I noticed at Seventh Fleet headquarters was coconuts all over the ground. Someone told me that this had been a coconut plantation. One cardinal rule over there was not to eat coconuts lying on the ground. You could eat the brown coconuts and drink the milk from the green coconuts, but if you ate a coconut off the ground, you would get what they called the screaming shits—the worst case of diarrhea you could imagine, just from eating a coconut off the ground. You quickly learned to knock them off the tree.

The next day after muster, the officer asked the four of us if we had driver's licenses. Al and Nap had driver's licenses, but Joe and I did not. Al and Nap were placed in the motor pool, and Joe and I remained with the group, which was otherwise all white. We were assigned to a large work party, which was split into two groups. Our task was to unload the ships that were bringing in the furnishings needed by Anchor Section. We were to work four hours on and four hours off, around the clock. These were the strangest hours of any work detail I had ever had. I found it amusing, even though we worked hard for several days.

I was assigned to a tent in which there was a Negro radioman second class. I was glad to see him; I had no idea that there were any other Negroes connected with Anchor Section other than steward's mates. Next to my cot was a foxhole dug by the person who had been here before me. The radioman taught me how to grab the mattress and roll over into it. You would land in the foxhole on your mattress. That was the easy part; the hard part was hoping like hell there were no snakes in that foxhole with you. I asked the radioman if he had ever messed up a message. He told me that there were ten radiomen taking the same message so there wouldn't be a fuck-up.

One day during my four hours off, I came back to the tent and the radioman was sitting on his cot, just staring. He wasn't looking at anything in particular. I talked to him, and he wouldn't answer. I went over and asked if he was all right; he still didn't answer. I was wondering, *What in the hell is wrong with this guy?* After a few minutes I decided to take him to sick bay, which was nearby.

The doctor asked, "What's wrong with this sailor?"

"Sir, I don't know. He won't talk; he's just been sitting around staring like that."

"What's this sailor's rating?" the doctor asked.

Even though I didn't see what difference this made, I told him: "Radioman second class."

"OK, then, there's nothing to worry about. He's just code crazy."

"What?"

"He's code crazy; it happens to radiomen. He's had too many dit-daw-dits. A little rest, and he'll be all right."

I left the sick bay thinking that war was the strangest situation a man could find himself in, and starting to wonder if I was going to survive.

One day all those who were motor machinists (we had no petty officers, only firemen) were called together and asked about any experience we had with the motors in landing craft. I happened to have the most experience, so I was chosen to be the engineer on the first boat acquired for the Anchor Section boat pool. There was a coxswain (third-class petty officer) already assigned to the boat. He was a tall, lanky blond white fellow from West Virginia named Wickline. The two of us were taken down the road about eighteen miles to a town called Tacloban. We took possession of an LCVP (landing craft vehicle, personnel) and returned to Toulousa by water. There was no dock to tie up to, so we had to anchor about a hundred yards offshore and wait for a "Duck" (amphibious truck) to come out and get us. This boat would be the workhorse for this base, and for us, too. We got supplies and ran a water-taxi service for ships that had no boats capable of landing on that beach. We ran day and night.

It didn't take long for Wickline and me to reach an understanding. On a trip out in Leyte Gulf, I asked him to shut the engine off so I could check the oil level while the engine was hot.

"No," was his response.

I turned the engine off and said to him, "I'm in charge of this engine. If I tell you to cut the engine off, cut it off, and if I tell you not to start the engine, don't start it. You can take this boat any place you want to, but it is my job to see to it that you get to where you are going, and don't you forget that."

Wickline said, "Look, boy! Do you want to swim back to the base? I'll throw your ass off this boat if you give me any more of your shit."

I had just pulled the oil depth gauge stick from the engine, and as I stood up straight I glanced toward shore. I guessed that we were about a half-mile offshore. I could swim a little, although long-distance swimming was not my line. I wasn't afraid of this guy—I wasn't afraid of any white man; a certain boxing champion had led me and all Negroes I knew to believe that no white man could beat a Negro. Still, there was a chance that this tall, lanky guy might do what he had said he would do. I checked the oil and said, "Let's go!"

When we had time off, I would go down to the main road and see the Filipinos. These people grew to an average height of five feet, were light brown in color, and had long straight jet-black hair. The hair of the women hung down to their hips. The first time I went down to the main road, it was apparent that the white Americans had communicated with the Filipinos and put the idea in their minds that Negroes were bad and should be avoided. At least they had done a pretty good job of blocking any chances the Negroes on this base might have had with the Filipino girls. I tried several times to talk to the women (twelve years old and up), to no avail. They would say, "You nigger, you bad." The Filipino men, on the other hand, were more than happy to talk to us. It was my firm belief that all Filipino men were pimps or con men. They were forever selling something or trying to con some American out of something he valued. There was no one crying in the Philippines.

All nonrated men had to stand guard duty at night on the beach behind the quarters of Admiral Kinkaid and his staff or in the village of Tolosa. The songs popular then were "I Walk Alone" and "Sentimental Journey." These songs were perfect for guard duty, because you had plenty of time to think while you walked. Walking guard on the beach behind Admiral Kinkaid's quarters at night, I often watched the Filipino girls and thought about how different they were from American girls. They would come down to the beach and obediently walk about five paces behind their American men for the entire four hours of their watch. They wouldn't disturb the men with talk or in any other way. The white American sailors were really captivated by these brown-skinned girls. I must admit that the Negro sailors also went for these girls, but they weren't fascinated by their color the way I believe the white guys were. The Negro sailors, being used to brown skin, weren't persuaded by color—just by sex.

One night I had guard duty in Tolosa with a white sailor. Our job was to keep all Americans out of the village after sundown. Right off the bat this sailor made it known that he didn't want to be with me. He said, "I'm going up to the beach, and I'll be back," and he left.

It was one of those rainy nights, so there were only a few people out. I walked up one street and down another, with no destination in mind—just waiting for twelve o'clock when I got off. Then I heard voices speaking English. I went over. I could tell it was a soldier by the raincoat. (The Navy didn't issue raincoats to its personnel; the Navy's only issue for rainy weather was the poncho.)

I said, "I'm sorry soldier, but no military personnel are allowed in the village after sundown. You will have to leave."

The soldier answered, "All right."

The voice came as a shock. I turned my flashlight onto the soldier's face. To my amazement, it was a woman. A white WAC! I was so stunned that I didn't know what to do. It was a standing order that no American woman was to be off her compound unless she had an armed escort.

Now, everyone—officers as well as enlisted men—violated rules. It's the way people acted when they had been under fire. War gave us all a "don't give a damn" attitude. You lived today, and to hell with tomorrow; today is yesterday's tomorrow. We didn't know when or if we were going to get out of the war. The only sure thing was that we were going to stay until it was over. In a situation like that, violating the rules was no big thing. So, here was this white WAC in the middle of a Filipino village, unescorted, on a dark rainy night. I decided not to worry about it. I walked away.

I got about thirty feet away and then turned around. What in the hell was this woman doing in this village at night?

I went back and asked her, "What are you doing in this village at night?"

She said, "I'm looking for the marketplace."

"What do you want to go to the marketplace for?" I asked.

"I'm supposed to meet someone there."

I said, "You know that you are not supposed to be out by yourself; military personnel are not allowed in this village after sundown. Now just who is it that you are supposed to meet?"

She said, "I'm supposed to meet my boyfriend at the marketplace at ten o'clock."

I really didn't believe her, but I played along. "Come on, I'll take you to the marketplace." We started walking, and I asked, "How did you get out without an escort?"

She was about to answer when a flashlight came on. I said, "That's my partner."

He came up, saying, "What have we got here?" He put the beam of his flashlight in her face and exclaimed, "By God, it's a white woman! What are you doing out here, honey?"

She answered, "I want to go to the marketplace."

He said, "Come on, honey, I'll take you."

I became a little angry at this guy. He had been wandering around by himself all night, and now he wanted to take this WAC where she wanted to go; forget about me. I decided to stay right with them because I didn't know what might happen, and I didn't want to miss anything. The three of us headed for the marketplace.

We arrived and went under the cover of one of the stalls, out of the rain. I said, "I don't see anyone down here."

The WAC said, "Give me your flashlight." I gave her mine, and she put the beam between two buildings; a jeep was parked there. We wouldn't have noticed it on our normal rounds.

I asked, "Do you know who that jeep belongs to?"

She answered, "Yes, it belongs to an Army officer who is in that house with a WAC."

I knew now why she was out tonight: her boyfriend was playing around on her.

She said, "Chase them out."

I went up to the hut and used my rifle butt to beat on the door. A Filipino man answered the door. I asked, "Is there anyone in here that's driving this jeep?"

At first he looked around, and then he said, "Yes."

An Army officer came out of a back room and said, "That's my jeep."

I said, "I'm sorry, but no military personnel are allowed in this village after sundown, so you will have to leave."

He said, "All right."

Returning to the stall in the marketplace, I saw the WAC and my companion in a tight embrace, lying on the stall. This was a helluva situation. The WAC was white, my companion was white, and I was Negro. It was the first time I had ever been in a situation like this with a white girl and a white man, but I was going to find out how far they were going to let me go. This guy couldn't beat me, so the only thing I was worried about was the WAC.

I sat on the stall beside them and said, "He's coming out."

They sat up, and we all watched the door of the hut. The officer came out, followed by a WAC. They got into the jeep and drove off toward the beach. My companion put his arm around the WAC. They lay back on the stall and resumed their smooching. I sat beside them swinging my rifle between my legs, looking out into the dark rain and occasionally looking down at them beside me. To be frank, I was just as excited as they.

After a short time the WAC sat up and said, "I want something to drink."

My companion said to me, "Yeah! How about you going to get a bottle?"

I said, "No, Dad, I put that officer and his girl out of that hut. *You* go get the whiskey."

He said, "Oh, all right, I'll go and get it." He got down off the stall and disappeared in the dark.

I asked the woman how she had gotten out of the WAC camp unescorted. She said, "I know the guard, and I just walked out." I asked what her name was and where she came from. She told me; we talked for a short while, then I laid my rifle on the stall and said, "Come here." She did, and we lay back on the stall.

My companion came back with the whiskey. The WAC and I sat up, and we all started drinking. This whiskey wasn't the same as in the States. It was a concoction made out of rice by the Filipinos, and they were selling it as fast as they could make it.

As we drank, we did some more smooching. That was as far as my companion and I got with the WAC. We walked her back to the WAC camp, and she said she would meet us at the marketplace the next evening.

We were there the next evening, but she didn't show, and the guards put us out of the village.

Since this was Seventh Fleet headquarters, it was only natural that one would see a lot of officers. This is the only time I was ever stationed at a base that had more officers than enlisted men. These officers ranked from admiral on down. One officer stationed here was the son of President Roosevelt.

Because of the great number of officers, there had to be a large number of stewards and steward's mates to serve them. This was also the first and only time I was stationed on a base that carried such a large complement of stewards and steward's mates. They accounted for one-third of the enlisted men on the base. It appeared to me that most of them were from the South.

I spent many days and nights talking to them. Some of the things they related to me concerning life in the Deep South were disgusting—just sickening. They told me about lynchings that never were recorded in police records and about the raping of Negro women, which seemed to be a favorite pastime of white men in the South; no white man was going to be convicted of raping or murdering a Negro. They told me how white men would come into the Negro districts, go into certain homes (already picked out), and take the daughters of a family or a man's wife and carry them off and rape them. Sometimes they didn't even bother to carry them off but raped them right in front of the crying mothers and the helpless fathers and husbands. They talked about how white men took Negro women for mistresses and forbade Negro men to associate with them. They talked about a Negro girl who went to the sheriff to report that she had been raped by some white men, and the sheriff told her to go on home before he locked her up. They went on and on, telling me of the animal-like acts of the white man in the Deep South. These things hurt me deeply, and I felt very sorry for my people in the South. But what could be done to end this sort of thing? The integration of the Navy might be the first step, but it was only one step, and we didn't even have any guidelines for it.

Then one day we received word that a dreadful thing had happened: President Roosevelt had died. His son left immediately for the States. I went down to the motor pool to see Al and Nap. We were the only three Negroes on the base who were not stewards or steward's mates (by this time Joe had received his Purple Heart and had been transferred out). We sat and talked, and it was our conclusion that the program to integrate the Navy would collapse; we had no faith in the haberdasher from Missouri who would now be running the country. We were anxious to find out exactly what would happen with integration, the Navy, and the country in general, now that President Roosevelt was gone.

There were also conversations in the boat pool office. The boat pool office was located in the signal tower down on the beach. Here all ships had to identify themselves upon approaching Leyte Gulf. The first time I went into the tower I felt very uneasy, for I was the only Negro there. I sat quietly and listened to everything that was said. It was a while before I said anything. To my surprise, the conversation there ran the same as any conversation. For some reason I had been expecting some talk that I wouldn't understand.

I remember one conversation where a signalman said, "During battle I stayed on the bridge."

I asked, "Don't you get under cover?"

The signalman said, "I'm not afraid, for the Lord will watch over me."

I said, "The Lord is watching over me too, but I'm going to help Him. He may take His eye off me for an instant, and that's all the time one needs to get killed out here."

There was a Jewish fellow there in the boat pool office. One day he took me off to the side where no one could hear what he had to say. He said, "Newton, we are in the same boat, you know. My people have been persecuted for over two thousand years."

I told him, "I understand that your people have been persecuted, but I also understand that the reason for your persecution and the reason for my persecution are very different. There is no Jewish race; it is only a religion. It is this religion that has been persecuted, not the people, whereas with me, it is my people that are being persecuted. All you have to do is change or fake a change in your religion, and you have ended your problem. You can still worship as you choose in private. I cannot change anything to get this shit off my back."

There was another guy there who said to me in a group conversation, "Say, Newton, suppose we built two trains exactly alike. Would you ride one while we rode the other?"

I said, "No! I want to ride the same train as you, for we are spending the same money, and I cannot see how you are better than I."

One day Wickline and I made a trip for the Officers' Club out to a ship to pick up some whiskey. The ship carried a cargo of only whiskey and beer. I hadn't known that the United States shipped this stuff in such great quantities. Upon returning to the base we came in with the tide. On this beach the waves broke high. No sooner had we landed on the beach than Wickline said, "I think we're in trouble." The waves were breaking over the stern of the LCVP and were turning us sideways on the beach, which is very bad. Wickline couldn't stop the boat from turning, nor could he back off, for the tide was pushing us farther up on the beach.

The officer in charge of the work party said to Wickline, "Drop the ramp, and we'll get as much of the cargo off as possible."

Wickline dropped the ramp, and the work party began to remove the cases of whiskey and throw them onto the beach. From the moment we hit the beach my job was at the seawater intake valve. These engines used seawater to cool the fresh water that cooled the engine. On the seawater valve there were two sea strainers. When one became clogged, you changed over to the other and cleaned the clogged one. Whenever one of those boats was on the beach, the engineer really had to work to keep those strainers clean. It took only a minute or two for a strainer to load up with the sand being churned up by the propeller. I could see Wickline from where I was cleaning the strainers. He was fighting the helm and shifting gears in an effort to right the boat. Wickline had a lock of hair that was forever falling down into his face, and he was constantly brushing it back with his hand.

Suddenly Wickline cut the engine off and said, "That's all, Newton, let's get out of this thing." We scrambled over the cases of whiskey and beer and waded ashore. The high surf began to take the LCVP under. The LCVP turned over onto its side, and the cargo of whiskey and beer spilled out into the water.

The officer in charge of the work party said, "You men can have whatever you can get. Be careful."

All the guys on the beach dove into the water as the LCVP slid under. I came up with five pints of rum.

The boat pool officer decided that the LCVP had been too small to do the job required. He sent Wickline and me to Tacloban to get an LCM (an LCVP could fit inside an LCM). This boat had twin engines and was very powerful. We could now handle any run, from supplies to recreation parties.

While we were in Tacloban, Wickline saw some guys do what we called "parking these LCMs," and he asked the guys to show him how to walk an LCM away from a pier or a ship. You put one engine in forward and the other engine in reverse, turned the wheel in the direction you wanted to go, and opened the throttle wide. The LCM would move sideways away from the pier or ship. When you were far enough away to not hit anything, you put the engine that was in reverse in forward, and the LCM would take off at full speed.

About this time I was given the opportunity to take the test for motor machinist's mate third class. I passed the test and was promoted to petty officer third class. Having a bigger boat meant more work. There were times when Wickline and I would be gone for a week at a time, and when we came in you would have thought we were pure bums, for we were unshaven, dirty, and ragged.

One evening a call came in from a destroyer requesting the use of the boat for a supply run early the next morning. We decided to go out to the destroyer that night and stay on board so that we would be there in the morning, ready to leave. We tied up to the stern of the destroyer and went on board. The officer of the day told Wickline, "You sleep in the seamen's compartment, and the colored boy can sleep with the steward's mates."

Wickline said, "He's not a steward's mate, and he sleeps where I sleep."

The officer said, "He cannot sleep with the white members of the crew."

Wickline answered, "Then we will sleep on our boat."

We climbed down onto our boat and went to sleep. The next morning we ate K-rations for breakfast, made the run, and returned to our base.

One day I was in my tent, and a Filipino girl came by and said, "Joe! You want a laundry girl, Joe? I do a good job, Joe." I looked at her, and that was about all there was to it. It was useless to try and guess her age, for they all aged very quickly in the jungle, and they started early.

I could have used a laundry girl; it was the fad. These girls were more than what the name implied. They did your laundry, cleaned your tent, and went to the movies with you, and they would sleep with you whenever you wished, for a little extra. A lot of these guys were going overboard for their brown-skinned lovers; they were sending home for women's clothes and stocking the girls' homes with food. Now I had a laundry girl, too.

My laundry girl and I became the best of friends, but there was something we had to get straight first: her. The Filipino girls were really putting something on the American servicemen as far as venereal disease was concerned. It seemed like every Filipino woman had a venereal disease of some type. The Clap Shack stayed loaded, even though we now had a medicine called penicillin that got rid of most VD in twenty-four hours. Penicillin was something the Japanese didn't have; we often discussed the health of the Japanese servicemen serving in the Philippine Islands.

Because of this, all our laundry girls were taken to sick bay before we would have sexual relations with them. Some of the girls resented this—but not nearly as much as we would have resented catching a venereal disease, which would have meant a medical record, a captain's mast, and a forfeiture of pay. We took the girls to sick bay at night and gave the corpsman 10 pesos ($5), and he would give them what we called a hot shot. It generally took four nights to be safe after the hot shot. Even then you couldn't bet on it, but you had done what you could.

Most of the time my laundry girl stayed at my tent when I was there. Sometimes I would stay at her family's house, although I preferred the tent with the cot and mattress to the bamboo floor in her house. It wasn't long, though, before she had a cot and mattress. I used to wrap her hair around my head at nights when we were alone. I could never get used to the smell of coconut oil, which all the Filipinos used. Coconut oil was something they just had to use. Perhaps they are still using it today.

One night I was staying at my laundry girl's house when a patrol from my base came by. I heard them talking outside: "If you see any of those niggers, shoot first and ask questions later."

There was no way I could get out of the house, and the patrol was coming in. I took off my shirt and threw it across the room. I grabbed my laundry girl, we lay on the floor, and I wrapped her hair around my head. We lay face to face as the patrol came into the room. They shined their flashlights on us for a few seconds and then left. That was one time when my color paid off; I was the same color as the Filipinos. The girl was crying when we sat up. I sat there with my arms around my knees, listening to the patrol make plans for their next check. They knew the houses where the Negroes' laundry girls lived, and they harassed them all the time. The answer to the question I had asked myself when they brought in that Japanese flyer had been confirmed.

All this time Wickline and I were busy running from ship to ship, hauling recreation parties and supplies and picking up dead bodies. Picking up dead bodies is no fun. You can smell a body for miles; the closer you get, the worse it smells. All the bodies we picked up were those of Americans or their allies. Many of them were drowning victims who had gotten caught in the heavy surf that pounded the beaches or had fallen off ships. The last one we picked up was a colored merchant seaman who had been reported as having fallen off the stern of a ship. We generally took two corpsmen with us on these body pickup runs. The corpsmen got the body out of the water and took it to sick bay for identification, determination of cause of death, and burial.

Wickline and I also went out regularly to Admiral Kinkaid's flagship, which was anchored a half-mile offshore; we would go out for various reasons, mostly to get fuel. On one occasion Wickline was off doing something, so I took a stroll around the ship. As I walked along the deck a heaving line missed me by a foot. A heaving line is like a clothes line with a lead weight on one end; it is tied to a heavy hawser line and is used for tying up on a pier or ship. I looked over the side and saw a fuel barge alongside. As I watched, a chief petty officer hollered, "Take a turn on that nigger head." I thought he was talking about me, and I left in a hurry. As I left, I heard them laughing, but the situation wasn't funny to me by any means. Later I found out that a nigger head is the part of a winch that does the work. You take a couple of turns around this part and start the winch, and it will pull. When I examined a winch one time, I found that the words *nigger head* were actually stamped into the part.

One day Wickline and I were in the boat pool office when one of the other guys in the boat pool came in. The first thing he did was hit me on the arm with his fist; he had a habit of doing this every time we met. This time I got mad and hit him in the jaw, and we started fighting. Now, this was right down my alley, for I didn't believe that any white man could beat me. As it happened, I did beat him. While I was checking the bruises I had gotten from the concrete floor, a white guy from one of the ships got into it.

He said, "You think you're smart, don't you?"

I said, "What did you say?"

He said, "You think you're smart."

I said, "You want to make something of it?" and we started fighting. Well, the guys in the office must have thought that we'd had enough fighting for one day, and they broke us up.

Another time Wickline and I were on our way up to the base. In order for us to get off the beach we had to walk down to a gate, because the area around the signal tower was also used for recreation parties from the ships. They would let these guys come ashore for some fun on land. They could do anything they wanted for a few hours—mostly drink beer; it was against Navy regulations to drink any alcoholic beverage on board ship. Another reason for fencing off the area was to prevent sailors from wandering off.

Wickline and I were crossing this area and were almost at the gate when a baseball just missed my head.

I said, "Hey, watch that ball."

The guy who had thrown it said, "Watch your head."

I started after him, but Wickline grabbed me and said, "Look, Newton, go on out the gate."

When I looked back, Wickline had the guy up over his head. He threw him to the ground, and then he came out the gate.

When he got outside he said, "Newton, let me tell you something. If you had gotten into a fight with that guy, you would have had that whole crew on you, and you can't beat them all. Remember that!"

As we walked up to the base I was thinking, *This guy's pretty strong, and I'd better be careful with him.*

Wickline and I were out on the bay several times during air raids. Guns would be going off, but we wouldn't stop until we reached our destination. We were told not to watch the sky because what goes up must come down, and sometimes there was a lot coming down around us. I liked to see those twin Bofors and those quad fifties fire, though, so I looked.

Wickline and I spent many days together. We drank from the same canteen, and sometimes we had the same women. During all the time we were together, we never discussed race. I don't know if we both consciously avoided it, but it never came up. The only thing I didn't like about Wickline was that lock of hair that was forever falling down into his face. He spent half his time pushing that curl back into place. I was tempted to cut that damn thing off a thousand times, but I never did.

Wickline wasn't the only one having trouble with his hair. There was no Negro barber on the base, and we had to do whatever we could to keep our hair manageable. Nobody had any clippers, so most of us used a razor blade on a comb. This was effective, but time-consuming. One of the steward's mates made a concoction called Conkaline. This stuff had a lye base and was dangerous to use. You could get a serious burn, or your hair might come out, but guys used it anyway because it would make your hair straight. After I started using Conkaline, I would kid Wickline that I had no curls to worry about.

Wickline and I were still having trouble whenever we landed the boat on the beach. Because of the heavy surf, we sometimes used a bulldozer to hold us steady while unloading, but this also caused a problem. It would take us so long to unload that we often found our boat high and dry; the tide would have gone out, and we would have to wait for high tide to get off the beach. Then someone came up with the idea of putting a large truck in the boat. The truck's weight would keep us steady and reduce the time we spent on the beach.

We would sometimes go out with the truck and a work party to Guiuan, Samar, our supply base, which was forty miles away. I never did figure out just how Wickline got us to Guiuan, because the compasses didn't work properly. They all were off, and if he made a wrong calculation we would be heading out into the Philippine Sea. He did it right, though, whatever it was; we made it to and from Guiuan every time.

One time we were returning in the dark. Someone yelled, "Hey, look!" We all looked to our right, and the bow of a ship was about fifteen feet from us. We were just starboard of the bow, and its wake pushed us away from the ship. We almost swamped because we were loaded. I looked at Wickline, who was busy getting the boat out of the wake and brushing that damn curl out of his face. Since we were still getting hit with air raids by the Japanese, everything was blacked out. With the clouds overhead, it was pure darkness. By the time the lookout on the ship spotted us and the ship's horn started blowing, we were well clear.

One day, coming into our base, we hit a piece of wood. Wickline and I both heard and felt it. I checked the engine room and saw no water, so I went back up with Wickline. I heard the exhaust bubbling, which meant it was under water. That meant we were taking on water. Again I checked the engine room and saw no water, so I checked the compartment behind the engine room, called the sternsheets. This was where the fuel tanks were located, and here I found the water. Wickline went ashore to inform the boat pool officer that we had a hole in the sternsheets and were taking on water. He told Wickline to take the boat to Tacloban; he would call and have another boat ready for us there.

Wickline returned to the boat and told me what the boat pool officer had said. I replied that we had better hurry, for water had started coming into the engine compartment. The water pump was located in the forward part of the engine compartment, but since the water was coming into the aft section, the pump was of no use. We got under way for Tacloban, eighteen miles away. I told Wickline, "Stay in close to the shore in case this thing goes down. If it does, we can swim ashore." He stayed in close, and we continued on our way.

After a while Wickline said he couldn't see. The boat's going down in the stern had made the bow rise, and he couldn't see over the big ramp on the front of this type of landing craft. I went forward, sat on top of the ramp, and guided Wickline with hand signals. When we reached Tacloban the stern of the boat was under water, and the water in the engine room was over the transmissions. They put a sling on the boat and pulled it out of the water with a big crane. We got a new boat and returned to our base.

The next day Wickline and I had to go to captain's mast to explain what had happened to the boat. The captain wasn't pleased with our explanation and gave us a warning. We didn't like that, but there was nothing we could do; we had to accept it.

Every morning when we were on the base, we had to go to formation. The officer of the day read the orders for the day, and he would read some rule or regulation, usually something along the lines of "Leave those Filipino girls alone." While he read, we would all stand there scratching. Everyone in the Philippines had what was called Jockey Itch. There was no cure, though if you went to sick bay they would give you a medication that burned like hell. It was comical to see everyone in formation scratching and the officer reading the orders of the day scratching.

One morning he read us a rule that nobody agreed with. It stated that if an American killed a Filipino, he would be court-martialed, but if a Filipino killed an American, he was simply to be regarded as uncivilized. The only good thing about this was that the Navy didn't have capital punishment. I knew that the Army did; I had seen notices tacked to trees saying some soldier was going to hang for something.

There was a Negro Army Engineer company about a quarter-mile down the road from our base. One night a Filipino man cut one of the Negro soldiers. The whole company went across the road to the village where he lived, looking for him. They didn't find him, so they leveled the entire village. I never found out if anyone got punished for that.

Meanwhile, another serious problem was developing on the base: the Navy was enlisting Filipino men right out of the jungle as steward's mates in the officers' mess. They couldn't speak English, which presented a problem in training them. But they were being put into the mess hall anyway while the Negroes were being taken out and assigned to clean the base.

The Negro steward's mates were mad about this, and they were getting very vocal. I told them that I would rather be cleaning up the base than waiting on officers, but they said no—waiting on officers was their job, and the Filipinos should be cleaning the base. Besides, as steward's mates these men had gotten used to eating what the officers ate; eating what the enlisted men ate in the general mess presented quite a change.

The situation continued. As more Filipinos came into the mess hall, more Negroes were moved out to clean up the base. Then one night when everyone was sleep there was a BOOM! I grabbed my rifle and hit the floor. I thought that a Jap patrol had gotten in, and so did the other guys who shared the tent with me. Then we heard men yelling and running toward the last row of dormitories. We got up and followed. It turned out that somebody had thrown a hand grenade into the Filipinos' dormitory. No one was hurt; the Filipinos didn't sleep in their dorm for fear of being attacked by the Negroes. (They stayed out in the jungle somewhere and reported for their watch at the officers' mess on time. We couldn't figure out how they told time, but they must have had some kind of system. Somehow they made it.)

The next night after everyone was asleep we heard the sound of machine-gun fire. This time everyone knew that the steward's mates were at it again. They raked the Filipinos' dorm from one end to the other with machine guns. Still no one was hurt.

The captain finally decided that he had had enough of this. First he put lights up in the row between the Negroes' dorms and the Filipinos' dorms and had armed guards placed along this row. This was to stop the harassment of the Filipinos by the Negroes. He then came up with a gem and started to transfer the Negro steward's mates over to the receiving station at Guiuan to await further transfer. As soon as a Negro was relieved of his duties in the officers' mess, he was transferred to Guiuan. This practice continued until the only Negroes left were the officers' cooks, officers' stewards, and a few steward's mates. When it was all said and done, I felt sorry for the steward's mates. The job of waiting on and cleaning up after officers was not for me. Maybe a few years earlier I could have done it, but that time had passed. As I have said before, a steward's mate was the lowest thing in the Navy; there was no doubt about it. I don't think it was a coincidence that the majority of the Negroes in the Navy were in its lowest classification.

The captain wasn't finished; he ordered all personnel sleeping in tents around the base to move into the dorms. I guessed his reason was that now there would be no sitting ducks in tents on the edge of the base if these Filipinos ever decided to get even. It also meant that there would be no more girls sleeping with me. I had to split up from the two guys I had been bunking with. They went into the steward's mates' dorm, and I got a bunk across from Wickline in the boat pool dorm.

One night Wickline and I were coming in from a run. We tied up to a mooring buoy a couple hundred yards offshore and signaled the tower to send the Duck to pick us up. No one came out. We continued to signal the tower, without getting any response, until a boat came by and gave us a lift onto the beach.

When we got to the beach, I could see the Duck and the driver standing next to it. While Wickline went into the boat pool office, I went up to the driver and said, "Didn't you see us blinking out there? Why didn't you come out and get us?" He didn't say anything, so I continued. "Don't you hear me talking to you, Mother Goose? Why in the hell didn't you come out there and pick us up? And what the hell you got on whites [white uniform] for?"

Then I noticed that there was an officer standing near the driver. The officer turned and said, "I'm sorry about that, son; I'm detaining him."

I looked at the officer, and in the dim light from the signal tower all I could see was stars. I wanted to rub my eyes, but I couldn't move. I wanted to disappear. This was an admiral! I let my eyes rise to his face in pure astonishment. I was face to face with the best-liked admiral in the U.S. Navy,

Admiral Halsey. All the guys said that they would give their left nut to serve under Admiral Halsey.

I said, "Yes, sir," saluted, and walked around the Duck. As soon as I was out of the admiral's sight I took off running down the beach. I don't know why; the only thing on my mind was the sight of Admiral Halsey. The driver of the Duck and I joked about this for some time. I found out that the admiral had been waiting for his boat; he was using one of those fast rescue boats as his barge.

Admiral Kinkaid was preparing to move his Seventh Fleet headquarters to Manila, but before the fleet left, they sent in the Shore Patrol and the Military Police. They locked up all the women and young girls and treated them for venereal disease. Twenty-five thousand females were treated the first day.

7 *Leyte*

The pace of the war was escalating; American troops were battling for control of Okinawa. The fighting was getting tougher, but the Marines were moving closer to the Japanese mainland. Everyone knew that the Japanese would fight harder there than anywhere else, but that seemed like the only way to end the war.

We got reports that we were losing more ships to the weather than to battles, but the Japanese really hammered our ships during the battle for Okinawa. They were using suicide planes called kamikazes. (The Japs may have gotten this idea from America. Early in the war, on 10 December 1941, an Army Air Force captain, Colin Kelly, dove his plane into a Japanese warship.) The carrier *Franklin* was so badly battered during this battle that the order was given to abandon ship. She didn't sink, though, and in the end every available man was used to sail her into Pearl Harbor; there she got another crew, which eventually took her to New York for repairs. The crew that brought her into Pearl Harbor was made up of stewards and steward's mates; they had been locked in the magazine, their general-quarters station, when the abandon-ship order was given. It is believed that if the *Franklin* had gone down when the abandon-ship order was given, these guys never would have made it. But instead of being casualties, they received medals.

Because of these losses, the Navy came back to its bases in the Philippines and elsewhere and took all available food supplies. To replace these supplies, we got a new canned meat being used by the military, called Spam. We had Spam every meal for a couple of weeks. I had Spam just about every way it could be fixed.

One day there was a lot of excitement on the base. We received word that America had dropped some fantastic bomb on the Japanese mainland, at a city called Hiroshima. This bomb was said to be the size of a basketball and capable of wiping out a whole city. It was called an atomic bomb. Nobody knew anything about this atomic bomb; we believed anything that was said about it. Three days later another atomic bomb was dropped on a city called Nagasaki.

That evening Wickline and I were sitting at the movie, listening to the records while we waited for the show to start, when the guy playing the records broke in over the PA system: "We have just received word that the Japanese have surrendered. There will be free beer and whiskey for the enlisted men at the Officers' Club."

All hell broke loose as men rushed to the Officers' Club. This was the beginning of the biggest party I have ever seen. Everyone was running and hollering; it was complete chaos. The war had ended! Ships in the harbor got into the spirit by firing their guns and shooting all kinds of flares into the sky. It wasn't quite dark, but they shot the flares anyway.

We arrived at the Officers' Club and started drinking whiskey as fast as we could. Officers, nurses, and WACs were all kissing. None of the nurses or WACS kissed me, but they kissed everyone else and just had a ball. This was the first and only time I ever legally got any whiskey on a naval base.

I don't know how long we stayed, but we drank a lot of whiskey, then Wickline suggested that we go up to the base. When we got there, he decided to go to the motor pool and get a Duck. We headed out on the road to Tacloban, which was so crowded that you could walk faster than the Duck could move; you couldn't make one mile an hour on that road. Every vehicle was overloaded. We were picking up any sailors and soldiers we saw. We didn't know who we had on that Duck, and we didn't care. Everybody was passing around cans of beer and bottles of whiskey. It had gotten dark now, and ships were still sending up flares in all the colors you could think of, just like the Fourth of July. It seemed as if integration had finally hit the services, for whites and Negroes were all mixed together celebrating on these vehicles. It was fantastic to see those thousands of soldiers and sailors having such a ball. It was great to be a part of it. The war was over, and we would be going home!

We couldn't get to Tacloban on that road, so Wickline took the Duck off the road and went down the beach. Somebody said we were coming to Red Beach, where the Army stored beer; Red Beach had been one of the landing places during the invasion of Leyte. We stopped alongside a stack of cases of beer; it must have been fifteen feet high, for we were on the Duck and still had to reach up to get beer. We had grabbed about thirty cases when shots rang out. The Military Police were shooting at us! Wickline took off up the beach and out into the water. The MPs came out into the water after us, still shooting. Wickline pulled the Duck back onto the beach, hit the road to Tacloban, and got us lost in the traffic. The MPs couldn't get to us through the crowd, so we managed to lose them. We went up the road toward our base giving cans of beer to anyone who wanted some.

Suddenly one of the guys in the rear said, "What's wrong with that soldier back there? He's been sitting back there on the tire since we left Red Beach. All through the shooting he was sitting on that tire."

The guy on the tire was a Negro. I asked him what was wrong.

He was holding his stomach. He looked up and said, "I've been hit."

I said, "Holy cow, this man has been shot, we got to get him to a hospital."

We were coming up to an Army hospital, but now nobody wanted to take this Negro soldier into the hospital for fear of getting into trouble; I mean, here we were with a load of beer, and this guy had been shot. Finally Wickline volunteered to take him in. We lowered the soldier down to Wickline. He carried him in his arms into the hospital, and we took off for the base. Wickline showed up a short time later and said he'd had no problem at the hospital; he just took the soldier in, told them he had been shot, and left. The party continued.

After a while I went over to the steward's mates' dorm. They were all out on the edge of the jungle, shooting their guns. They had all kinds of guns: machine guns, carbines, and forty-fives. I got a carbine and emptied a clip into the jungle. Then I walked out in front of all that shooting and went to see my laundry girl.

When I got to her house, I saw no one. I mean, the entire settlement was gone; I was the only person around. Where was everybody? I kept calling, and finally my laundry girl showed up, scared to death. I could tell just by looking at her that she was frightened.

"Where is everyone?" I asked.

"They leave; Japanese come back, much fighting."

"No, the Japanese aren't back. The war's over; the Americans are doing all the shooting. The lights in the sky are from us, we're having a big party. The war's over; the Japanese quit, they're gone for good." I almost got sober trying to make her understand what was going on.

She said, "Japanese no more?"

I said, "Yeah, Japanese no more."

She turned and started calling some names, speaking in her language. I understood some of what she was saying; she was saying it was all right to come out. People began coming out of the jungle, where they had been hiding. Some of them ran off and returned with rice whiskey; others had that nasty-tasting jungle juice called Tuba. We just drank and partied the rest of the night. I woke up in my laundry girl's house. That was some night!

I went back to the base for breakfast, but there were no cooks. Everyone was wandering around drinking and glad to be going home soon. This celebration lasted for three days.

Guys were being sent home on a point system. You got so many points for service time, so many for being overseas, and so many for being married. I figured my points out and found out that it would be two years before I got sent home.

Whenever someone got orders to go home, there was a party. There was one party that I doubt will ever be beat; it was also the strangest. One homosexual white sailor was so happy to be going home that he attempted to have oral sex with every man on the base. He started at the first dorm on the first row, and tried every man on the base. He didn't succeed with all of them, however, and was beaten very badly before it was over.

I had a lot of time to think during all these celebrations. There was one coincidence that especially grabbed me. When the word came over the radio that the Japanese had bombed Pearl Harbor, I was sitting in a movie theater in Baltimore. No announcement was made in the theater. When I left the theater around 3 P.M., I looked up and down Pennsylvania Avenue, the main street for Negroes in Baltimore; it was deserted. I wondered where everyone was, and I didn't see anyone on the entire trip home. When I entered my house, two of my brothers (who were in the National Guard) were putting on their uniforms. I asked where they were going. They told me that the Japanese had attacked Pearl Harbor, the president had declared war on Japan, and they had been ordered to report for duty. They left Baltimore the next day. Then when the war ended, I was once again sitting in a movie theater, this time ten thousand miles away from Baltimore. In a sense, for me the war began and ended in a movie theater. I wondered if anybody else had been in the same situation.

About this time I developed terrible pains in my stomach. I went to sick bay, and they sent me to the same Army hospital where we took the Negro soldier who had been shot the night the war ended. I was sent to the surgical ward. The doctors suspected that I had appendicitis, but after another examination they found that I had acute gastritis. The Army guys thought they served good food in that hospital, but I thought it was terrible. After the second day I got out of my bed and returned to my base to eat, then went back to my bed; canned beef and boiled eggs were not my idea of good food.

I had been in the hospital for two weeks when one night at about nine o'clock a jeep pulled up to the tent where I was. A couple of guys from the boat pool came in.

I said, "Hey there."

They didn't say anything until they were at my bedside, then one said, "Newton, we got some bad news for you."

I didn't have any idea what he was going to say. I asked, "What's that?"

He said, "Wickline just drowned."

I jumped up out of bed and hollered, "What?"

The guy said that Wickline and some other guys from the boat pool had taken an outrigger (a Filipino boat) out to our LCM, which was loaded with beer, to get a couple of cases. Wickline fell off the outrigger and drowned.

I put on my clothes, and we left for the beach.

When we got to the beach the guys were still giving Wickline artificial respiration. We stood there watching as they worked on him. That damn curl was hanging down in his face. When the base doctor came, he turned Wickline over onto his back and examined him. After a while he said, "He's dead."

I said, "Oh, no, are you sure he's dead?"

The doctor repeated, "He's dead."

I went over and knelt down beside Wickline and shook him, saying, "Come on, Wickline, get up," but he wouldn't move. For some reason, I don't know why, I slapped him as hard as I could, but he still wouldn't move.

The doctor said, "It's no use; he's dead."

They put Wickline's body in an ambulance and took him to the base sick bay. I followed in a jeep. When we got to sick bay the base commander came up. He and the doctor got into an argument.

"This man drowned trying to steal beer," the captain was saying, waving his finger in the doctor's face. "He fell into the water, and couldn't swim; that's how he drowned. The men with him saw him fall into the water. They said he came up once, smiled at them, and went back under. That's when they realized that he couldn't swim and went in after him. They managed to get him to shore, but as you can tell, it was too late. You pronounced him dead. He died of his own negligence, and that's how it's going into his records."

"Nobody over here dies of his own negligence as long as I'm the doctor. I don't care who it is or how he dies—it's in the line of duty as far as I'm concerned."

The captain looked at the doctor, then turned and walked away without responding.

Still not wanting to believe it, I asked the doctor, "Is he really dead?"

He said, "He's dead; we'll bury him tomorrow. Don't bother me any more about it."

I had thought Wickline could swim. He never said he couldn't; when we took that sinking LCM down to Tacloban, he gave no indication that he couldn't. I walked away, and the guys took me back to the hospital. I didn't sleep that night for thinking about Wickline, my buddy.

The next day I dressed and went back to my base for Wickline's funeral. His body was taken to Tacloban to be buried in the American military cemetery. They asked me if I wanted to carry the casket. I told them that I could hardly walk, so I walked behind the casket. There was a graveside service, performed by a chaplain.

As they lowered Wickline's body into the ground, I saluted and said, "So long, buddy." Then we left.

When we got back to the base, I went to the dorm and pulled out Wickline's footlocker. I began to take out all his personal things, thinking that I would take them to his family in West Virginia. Then I started thinking of what the consequences might be if I showed up in West Virginia with his belongings. It might not be as good an idea as I thought. Wickline was white; I did not know how his people would take it when I, a Negro, told them what had happened. For some reason they might blame me, even though I hadn't even been with him when he drowned. I opened a pack of Wickline's cigarettes and lit one as I sat on his cot and thought. I came to the conclusion that I had better leave well enough alone; "died in the line of duty" was perhaps better than what might happen to me if I went to West Virginia. I closed Wickline's footlocker and shoved it back under his cot. I thought that this was indeed a funny world. Simply because I was a Negro and he was white, I was prohibited from doing anything for him. Even in death I couldn't do anything. I made up my mind that I was not ever going to let anyone else get as close to me as Wickline had been.

I returned to the hospital. It was two weeks before I got out. By that time they had removed all of Wickline's things.

When I returned to the boat pool, I put in for a transfer. I didn't feel right about being there anymore, even though I knew everybody. The transfer came quicker than I had expected; I guess the officers understood how I felt. I was transferred to the base motor pool. When I reported, Nap and Al were still there. They shared a tent on the road and had converted part of it into a bar. The tent had been partitioned; Nap and Al slept on one side of the partition, and the bar was on the other. On the side of the tent facing the road there was a sign over the door that read "Fools Rush Inn." The bar had three tables and a bar with a few stools. They told me they had some parties in there after work, drinking stateside liquor or Grade A 190-proof alcohol, and they always had ice-cold beer, which was a luxury. Being in a motor pool, a man finds out that he has friends he has never seen before.

The motor pool officer told me that even though I was rated, I had to start on the tire rack, like any other new man in the motor pool. When he showed me the tire rack, I thought that there must not have been a new man in the motor pool for some time. Tires were stacked head high, and there were rows and rows of them, all flat. There were all kinds of tires here—truck tires, jeep tires, Duck tires, and automobile tires for the cars used by high-ranking officers. Most of the tires had rims holding them on, and I was working with an air compressor that had no gauge. Every time I blew one up, I worried that the damn rim would come off and go right around my neck, but that never happened. I went to work on these tires. The strangest thing to me was that 90 percent of these flats had been caused by nails. How could people find enough nails in the jungle to cause this many flats?

The tire rack was just what I needed. Wickline's death had really upset me, and this job took my mind off my grief. Working with the air compressor, I had no time to worry about Wickline.

The whole routine of life in the motor pool was good for me; it never closed. There were drivers and a dispatcher on duty twenty-four hours a day. Those who were on duty from midnight to four in the morning got sandwiches at midnight. One night Al, Nap, and I were up at midnight in the dispatcher's shack, and the duty driver went to the mess hall for sandwiches. He was gone so long that we were wondering about him. He returned saying that some nigger stole his jeep. Nap pulled him out of his seat and hit him; he went right through the plywood wall. He came back in and said he was sorry for what he had said, and that was that.

USO shows had started to come to the island. The military had a strange way of organizing these things. When a show came, the Air Force took care of the quarters and meals, and the Navy furnished the transportation. The first show we had was called "Lucky Seven," an all-Negro show. It was five girls and two men. In this group was an act called Freddie and Flo, which I had seen several times on the stage of the Royal Theater in Baltimore. Al and Nap were the drivers for the group, so they came over to the Fools Rush Inn after they had completed their shows for the day. We were all drinking ice-cold beer and Grade A 190 alcohol and Coke or juice. The stewards were bringing over steaks and other food from the officers' mess. We had a ball! This was the first time I'd had a chance to talk to any Negro American civilians since speaking to those Negro Red Cross workers down in New Guinea. It was good just to see them, talk to them, and smell their perfume. I guess it was the first time some of them had drunk Grade A 190 alcohol; it really wasn't bad, but you had to mix it.

Not long after the Lucky Seven left, Nap received his orders to go home. That was the excuse for another big party. We had all we wanted to eat and drink, and all the women we wanted, too. This party was for motor pool personnel only, and it went on all night. We sent Nap off in style! After he left, I moved from the boat pool dorm into the Fools Rush Inn.

One day the motor pool officer asked me to make a trip, but I told him I didn't know how to drive. Well, it turned out that all motor pool personnel had to be able to drive. The motor pool officer could have transferred me, but instead he had one of the white drivers teach me. I had my license within a week, but I could only drive light vehicles.

Another large USO show came, the Broadway musical *Oklahoma!* It was a large show. They were to do only one show in the area. All the ships around sent their crews ashore; it was the largest crowd I have ever seen at a show anywhere. This was my first time seeing a Broadway production, and I was never so completely entertained. Everyone agreed that *Oklahoma!* was the greatest show that ever came overseas.

A few weeks later Tiny Bradshaw and his band came. They were going to be in our area for five days doing shows each night at various places. I had known of Tiny before I joined the Navy. There was a girl singer, Saundra Lee, with his band. I don't remember any of the songs she sang. Whenever she appeared on stage I would be sitting there with my eyes batting like a frog in a sandstorm. This woman had everything a man could ask for, and all the troops were letting her know that. The last song Tiny Bradshaw did on each show was "Make the San Fernando Valley My Home." He changed the words to "Make the U.S.A. my home." It was done with a jazzed-up, fast beat. When the guys left the show, they would be dancing and singing, "Make the U.S.A. my home."

Al had Saundra Lee and some members of the band come up to the Fools Rush Inn after the first show. The party was on again, with the stewards bringing over the food and good ol' Grade A 190. The next day Saundra Lee and a tenor sax player with the band, Count Hastings, came back to the Fools Rush Inn and spent the day, then they went back to the Air Force base in the evening to get ready for the next show. This became a part of their routine.

One day we were sitting around drinking beer, and Count Hastings asked if we had heard the new tune that was out, "How High the Moon."

I told him, "We don't hear anything over here except that crap that GI Jill puts out. She is the saddest thing alive."

He had a piccolo in his pocket. He took it out and played "How High the Moon."

On their last night, after the last show, we were in the Fools Rush Inn talking, and we decided to take them to a beer hall run by the Army, where troops could buy beer and listen to records. Saundra Lee, Count Hastings, Al, and I got into a carryall (a vehicle like a big van) and headed to the beer hall. Everyone knew who Saundra was from seeing her perform at the show. People kept sending cases of beer to our table; Al and I would put the beer in the carryall.

Everyone was having a good time until two white MPs came up to the table. One of them said, "No civilians allowed in here."

I said, "These are Americans. That rule is for Filipinos."

He said, "No civilians allowed. They have to leave."

The MPs were armed, so we decided to leave. As we got into the carryall, about seven or eight white soldiers came out and got into a weapons carrier nearby. I don't know if anyone else noticed this; I paid it no mind.

We headed for the Fools Rush Inn. We had passed through a little village called Palo and were running alongside the Palo airfield. It was pitch black; the only lights were from vehicles on the road. A vehicle coming up on the outside bumped the carryall and forced Al to run off the road. It was the same weapons carrier with the white guys in the back. We knew what was happening, and we had no guns.

While we were still running off the road, Al thought fast. He made a circle and headed back toward Palo. He switched off the headlights and put on the convoy lights, which gave just enough light to see about twenty feet ahead. Using convoy lights, you couldn't be seen from the air—or from behind either, since the tail lights would also be off. But the guys in the weapons carrier realized that we were going the other way; we watched as they turned around.

Palo was about a half-mile down the road, and we had a lead of about two city blocks. When we got to Palo, Al turned onto the first little street. Of all the damn luck, it dead-ended a hundred yards from the road.

Someone in the carryall said, "This is it."

We came to stop. Al, Count Hastings, and I got out and left Saundra Lee in the carryall. We went around to the rear of the carryall and stood looking up the street. We didn't say anything, and believe it or not, I wasn't scared. As we stood there, waiting, the weapons carrier sped past. We rushed back into the carryall, Al turned it around, and we again headed for the Fools Rush Inn, now about three miles away, to get our guns.

When we pulled up in front of the Fools Rush Inn, Al and I jumped out and ran inside. I got my carbine, Al got his forty-five, and we ran back outside. We put Saundra Lee and Count Hastings in the beam of the headlights. We wanted the guys in that weapons carrier to see Saundra Lee; if they came and saw her and got out of that weapons carrier, they were going to die "in the line of duty." I leaned on the fender with my gun, and Al was looking down the road with his gun in his hand. But we never saw the weapons carrier again, and after fifteen minutes we went inside for a much-needed drink. The Tiny Bradshaw Band left the next day for Manila and perhaps Tokyo. We wished them happy landings. One thing I hadn't understood in New Guinea was why American women in a war zone were always accompanied by armed guards. Now I understood and agreed 10,000 percent.

Orders came to close the naval base at Tolosa, Leyte. All personnel and equipment were to be transferred to the naval base at Guiuan, Samar. Any equipment that was not serviceable was to have the carburetors, starters, and generators removed and be left behind. All those tires I had repaired were stacked on trucks for shipment to Guiuan. Rows of airplanes were left on the Palo airstrip.

Before we left we had one last party at the motor pool. They brought in some girls, and we had grilled steaks, beer, and good ol' Grade A 190. I was at the grill getting a steak when one of the white guys from the motor pool came up to me and said, "Newton, I want to tell you something."

I looked at him and saw he was pretty well loaded. "Yeah, what's that?"

He said, "You are a good nigger. You are the best damn nigger I ever met."

This shocked me. I said, "What?" I looked at him. I didn't know if I should knock him on his ass or what, so I just turned around and walked away. My father always said that whatever you do, be the best, but I am quite sure being "the best nigger" was not what he meant.

This word *nigger* is a funny word. It can be acceptable, depending on how it is used, when it is used, the tone it is used in, and, most important, who is using it. *Nigger* would not be acceptable, even when used by another Negro, if used with the wrong tone or in the wrong place. This was the first time a white man had stood in my face and called me a nigger. I guess he had the right tone. Then again, "Smile when you say that."

A few days later we drove all the vehicles we were going to carry down to the beach and put them on board a waiting LST. All of the people who lived around there were on the beach to see us go. There was a lot of crying on the beach, and on board the LST too, for a lot of the guys didn't want to leave their girls. I gave my laundry girl some money and kissed her goodbye. She said she was going to follow us in an outrigger. I told her it would take many, many days for us to get there on a big ship, so she would never make it.

When I boarded the LST, I went on deck with everyone else. The Filipinos were singing a song to the tune of "You Are My Sunshine," but they changed the words and said *sunki* instead of *sunshine. Sunki,* in their language, meant friend. The LST pulled away. Goodbye, Leyte; hello again, Samar.

Things on Samar had changed quite a bit since I had last been stationed there. The Filipinos had come back out of the hills, and the town of Guiuan was bristling with people going about their business. I was bunked in a hut on the edge of the base with three other guys. One night we had just returned from visiting some girls out in the jungle and had started to play cards. We looked up, and there were two white fellows standing in the doorway with submachine guns.

One of them said, "Come on."

I said, "What's going on?"

"Don't ask any questions. Come on. All of you are under arrest."

I said, "What the hell is going on here?"

He said, "Out." They put us in a truck and took us to the brig.

When we got inside the brig, I noticed that most of the Negroes on the base were there, and others were still being brought in.

I said, "What in the hell is going on around here?"

One of the guys said that a white sailor had shot a Negro sailor over a Filipino girl, and the Negro sailors were starting to riot up at the supply depot, so they were locking up all the Negro sailors on the island.

I said, "Now ain't this some shit." I had heard about the incident earlier; everyone knew about it, but nobody was upset. I was starting to get upset at being locked up, though. A white sailor shoots a Negro sailor, and they lock up all the Negro sailors—that's bullshit.

Sometime later that night I called the guard and told him I had to take a leak. He opened the door, and we went out. Once we were outside he said, "Nigger, you better piss or I'm gonna blow your head off."

I looked at him, some young punk with a submachine gun that was bigger than he was. He continued to call me all kinds of nigger. Now this was a situation where that word *nigger* hurt. Every time he called me a nigger it was like getting hit with a lash. I didn't want to get this guy so excited that he would pull that trigger, so I said nothing and managed to take a leak. We went back into the brig. I was thinking if I ever caught that bastard when this was over, I would break his neck.

The next day we were released. I heard there had been some trouble up at the supply base, but everything had cooled off. The captain ordered all tents torn down, and we moved into a dorm with the mess attendants. Now, I was not a mess attendant. I should have bunked with the Engineering Division on the base, as the white engineers did, but discrimination was prevalent here. Once again, who would listen to my complaints?

One night while we were talking, some of these guys were singing the songs they used to sing while working on the railroad, fixing rails and ties. Some white guy came into the dorm hollering, "Knock it off. It's after taps; go to sleep."

A hail of shoes flew at him, and he ran out. A short time later a truck backed up to the dorm—those white guys with submachine guns again. It was "Everybody out" and into the truck and off to the brig again.

The officer of the day was at the brig. He wanted to know who had started throwing the shoes. No one said anything, so he told us that we were going to stay in the brig until he found out. Finally one guy said he was the one who had started throwing the shoes. The officer of the day let the rest of us go. He said that he was holding the other guy for captain's mast the next day. Nothing happened to him at captain's mast.

Now, one thing seemed to be a fact: whenever any trouble started over there, the Negro Navy man was the first to suffer. Those whites were too quick to pull out machine guns. Someone was bound to get hurt if they kept it up. They were going to start something that machine guns couldn't quell.

In January 1946 I received orders to go home. I packed my gear and boarded the ship. This ship had a crew of merchant seamen; Navy crews never could stand merchant seamen. The ship was loaded with returning servicemen, plus some Filipino mess attendants who couldn't speak English. We had twenty-one days of daydreaming about what we were going to do when we got out of the service, and twenty-one nights of gambling. On the crap tables, one roll of the dice could cover the price of mink coats, big cars, houses, and businesses. Thousands of dollars changed hands at the roll of the dice.

Two days before we were to arrive at San Francisco, the captain came on the PA system and said that all gear was to be searched; no guns or pets were to enter the United States. There was a mad rush by most of the guys to get to their gear. I threw my carbine over the side. But the search never took place.

It was late evening when we saw the lights of San Francisco. The captain came on the PA system to announce that we were going to anchor off San Francisco for the night and go ashore in the morning. That was the longest night of my life. All night long we sat on deck, looking at the lights of San Francisco. The next morning we weighed anchor and sailed into San Francisco Bay. We were met by a boat carrying a band and a load of girls as we passed under the Golden Gate Bridge. After tying up to the pier, we boarded buses to take us to the naval base on Treasure Island.

Upon arriving at Treasure Island, we were all called around an officer who told us that they had no room for us to sleep on the base. Liberty would therefore start immediately for those who wanted it. We were given uniforms and put on the streets of San Francisco without even a short-arm inspection.

The first thing I did was to go to a barbershop. I hadn't had a real barber touch my hair since I left, almost two years before. Then I went to find my friend. She was living in the same place, but when she opened the door I was shocked. Here was a dirty, half-dressed winehead. The apartment was only half-filled with furniture; another winehead female was slouched in a chair in the kitchen. I kissed my friend, told her I was on my way to the East Coast and didn't have any time, gave her $50, and left. Then I went around the corner and found a woman. We celebrated my return to the States. The song played on the jukebox the most that night was "I Cover the Waterfront."

I returned to Treasure Island the next day, only to be told that I was not on draft to leave. I headed back to San Francisco. This went on for three or four days before I was told that I was to leave by train for the naval separation center at Bainbridge, Maryland.

8 Back Home

I was to leave for Bainbridge on a troop train; it was loaded with guys going home. Unlike the train that first took me to the West Coast, this one had dining cars. We only had to stop to change engines or to take on water and food. Sometimes during these stops we had time to make it to a liquor store. The trip to Bainbridge took us four days.

Bainbridge had been a naval training base during the war; after the war ended it was used as a separation center. At Bainbridge I received my first physical since I had been in the hospital on Leyte. It took three or four days to get processed out of the U.S. Navy. On 24 February 1946, as I walked out of the gates of Bainbridge, I was still mad that I had thrown my carbine into the Pacific Ocean; no one had searched any of my gear.

When I arrived home I found out that my grandmother had died in New Jersey. Most of the family had left for the funeral. I left for New Jersey early the next morning. When I got there, my mother didn't recognize me; I was about five shades darker than when I had left for the South Pacific. The funeral served two purposes: I had the opportunity both to bid farewell to my grandmother and to see all the family and friends. I learned that my friend Eddie, whom I had left in San Diego, had what we in the Navy called "good duty." He was traveling all over the United States, escorting the bodies of fallen Navy men home to their loved ones.

The changeover from military man to civilian is not an easy process. I was so used to being told what to do that I couldn't seem to act on my own. Some guys can make the adjustment very quickly; for others it takes a long time.

There were no jobs to be had, and like everybody else I knew, I went down to the unemployment office and signed up for the Fifty-two Twenty Club. This wasn't really a club; it was $20 a week for fifty-two weeks—the standard unemployment benefit. I was given a form to fill out that asked everything except the name of the doctor who had delivered me. I put down diesel mechanic as my occupation.

The woman behind the counter looked at my form. "If you don't change your occupation, you'll never get a job," she said. She had the tone of one of those people who can always tell you what's best for you to do. I had already decided that I didn't like her.

"What do you mean by that? I'm not changing my occupation; I'm a diesel mechanic. That's what I was trained to do, and that's what I've been doing for the last three years."

"There are no jobs for Negro diesel mechanics. You'd better change your occupation."

"Well, you might as well give me my fifty-two checks now, because I'm not changing it." I turned in my form and left. That woman had gotten under my skin. I was going to prove to her that a Negro could get a job as a diesel mechanic.

I applied first at the two railroads that passed through Baltimore. The answer was no. I went to a large company that built diesel equipment for construction and got the same response. I went to the U.S. Civil Service; on the board there was a notice that they were taking applications for diesel mechanics at the U.S. Navy testing center at Annapolis, Maryland. Annapolis was only about thirty miles from Baltimore, so I went down to the testing center and got an application. The man giving out the applications told me not to bother to send it in. As much as I hated to admit it, the woman at the unemployment office had been right.

Just as an example of how things were, my sister had to have some medical assistance, so she went to the hospital. She had to fill out a form so that the hospital could figure out how much she had to pay.

The woman asked her, "Are you working?"

My sister said, "No."

"Are you married?"

"Yes."

"Does your husband work?"

"No."

"Where do you live?"

"With my mother and father."

"Do they work?"

"No."

"Do you have any sisters or brothers?"

"I have one sister and four brothers."

"Do any of them work?"

"No."

The woman said, "On your next visit we might have some plan worked out for you to pay this bill."

That was the way it was in Baltimore in 1946: no jobs. Somehow we got by.

Even though no one was working, we still managed to have a good time. There were drinking parties almost every night, somewhere. Although what we were drinking was wine, we still had a ball.

I finally found a job as a waiter in one of the private Jewish clubs. I didn't care for this type of work, but I made more than $20 a week. The job showed me just what went on in these private clubs. I must admit, I was amazed at some of the things I saw. For example, one night I was coming through the dining room carrying a tray of nine steak dinners. As I was moving along the porch, a woman seated at a table turned around in her seat. As she did, she stuck her leg out, and I tripped. The steak dinners went down on the floor.

The headwaiter rushed over and said, "Hurry up and get this up off the floor."

I told him, "Get it up yourself—I quit," and I went back into the kitchen.

The headwaiter came into the kitchen after me, trying to get me to stay, but I refused. While we were talking the busboy came into the kitchen with the dinners I had dropped on the floor. The chef told the busboy to bring the steaks to him. He took a towel, wiped each steak off, put them on the grill, turned them over, put them on plates with the trimmings, and sent them right back out to the party that was waiting for their dinners.

I walked out. Back to the Fifty-two Twenty Club.

It was summer, and all I was doing was drinking wine on the corner with the fellows; there was nothing else to do. The drugstore where we bought our wine had a sign on the wall that read "A Day without Wine Is Like a Day without Sunshine," and I was starting to believe it. All the fellows on the corner agreed that there was something called "Fight Your Grandmother" in the wine we were drinking; it made you do strange things. I made up my mind that I had to get away from this situation, so I went down and reenlisted in the Navy.

It was 13 August 1946. I had been out too long to get the shipping-over pay, and I didn't want to go through boot camp again. The recruiting officer said I wouldn't have to go through boots, and I would keep my third-class petty officer rating. I was sent to the U.S. Navy receiving station at Anacostia, Virginia, which was just over the Potomac River from Washington, D.C. Here I had a physical examination and went through the other procedures for in-processing, except I was not issued any Navy clothing. I was told that I was not eligible under the Navy regulations to receive another issue of clothing. I told the officer that I had been out longer than the ninety-day reenlistment period, and because of this I was a new enlistment. Two days later they decided that they'd better give me an issue of clothing, or I was going to be the only Navy man on that station walking around in civilian clothes.

A few days later I was transferred to the Naval Gun Factory across the river in Washington, to await transfer to a permanent assignment. I reported to the officer of the day at the Naval Gun Factory and gave him my orders and my records. He had a first-class petty officer explain what I was supposed to do during my stay. The petty officer took me to a yeoman in the outer office and had my liberty pass typed up. He gave me the pass and told me that all petty officers had liberty every night and every weekend. I told him I wasn't interested in going on liberty right then; I wanted to get readjusted to Navy life, and I was broke. He told me to keep the pass as long as I was at the Naval Gun Factory. This was the first base I had been on where I had liberty every night and every weekend. This was starting to look like good duty.

The dormitory I was to stay in was a three-story building, if you include the basement, where the Negroes bunked; the white sailors had the other two floors. As I looked around that basement I thought to myself that the integration of the U.S. Navy hadn't reached Washington yet, even though this was where it had all started. As far as I could determine, the integration of the Navy had been unsuccessful. Here I stood in the nation's capital, and the same things that I had faced when I first entered the Navy three and half years before still confronted me. It was sickening to think that President Roosevelt's order to integrate the Navy had not traveled over a mile in three and a half years. They had taught us that we had to be smart and use our heads, that we had to be better than good to compete with white sailors. But why? What good was it if the leaders of our nation didn't back us up? As far as I could see, we were still at day one.

In front of this dorm were two cannons from some bygone period in history. I was given a detail to shine these cannons every Friday for the inspecting officer. The U.S. Navy must have spent a fortune shining those cannons. It didn't take a can of metal polish to shine them; it took many cans. After the inspection I could go on liberty.

One Saturday I decided to go to Baltimore for the weekend. When I returned, the first-class petty officer was looking for me.

"Newton, you have captain's mast. You were reported absent without leave."

"I wasn't AWOL. You've got the wrong guy. I have liberty every weekend."

"No, you don't have liberty every weekend."

"You told me yourself, when I first got here, that I had liberty every night and every weekend."

"You must have misunderstood. You have liberty every *other* night and every *other* weekend."

I said, "Bullshit! You told me I had every night and every weekend off."

He said, "I know that's what I told you, but you don't. That's just the way we've been working it. If you go up to the captain and tell him that you were told that you had every weekend off, you'll mess it up for everyone else."

I could see that when he said "mess it up for everyone else," he meant himself, too. If I told the captain that this guy had been giving every petty officer every night and every weekend off, nothing would happen to me, but he could be busted to second class, or get brig time or be transferred.

I said, "Ain't this a damn shame? You get me into something, then ask me not to get out of it. Just what in the hell am I going to tell the captain? He's going to hang my ass, and you know it. Get out of my face, you son of a bitch."

He said, "Well, it's all up to you."

I went to captain's mast, and the captain asked me why I had been absent. I didn't know what to say, even though I had thought all night about what I was going to tell him. I knew it was no use, so I said, "I went to Baltimore and met a girl, and I got tied up, and I couldn't get back."

The captain said, "Ten days in the brig."

I said, "Yes, sir!" I saluted, left the room, and was escorted to the brig.

The brig in Anacostia was unlike any other brig I had ever heard of. Everything a prisoner did was done on quick time. I mean, everything you did, you had to run. Whenever you went out, a Marine guard would call your name. You would run to the guard and give your full name, service number, the number of the cell block you stayed in, and your brig number. As you might expect, I had a little trouble at first remembering all those numbers. Every time you missed a number, you got kicked in the ass. It didn't take long for me to memorize all the numbers. After all that running in the brig, I was in good shape, too.

There was a sailor in a cell by himself who had shot and killed several of his shipmates with a submachine gun somewhere in China. All he ever did was read the Bible. I remember thinking that if he had picked up his Bible instead of that submachine gun, those guys would still be alive. The U.S. Navy didn't have capital punishment, but he took care of that for them. After I had been in the brig a few days, he hanged himself.

Finally my ten days were up, and I was returned to the Naval Gun Factory only to find that I was on draft for Norfolk, Virginia. My orders read that I was to report to the U.S. Navy base at Norfolk, and then to the commanding officer of the USS *Donner*, LSD 20.

9 *USS Donner*

I really was happy now that I had finally been assigned to a seagoing ship. The last ship I had been assigned to was a YNG at San Diego. That ship didn't go anywhere, though; she just opened and closed the antisubmarine nets to the harbor. I arrived at the Norfolk naval base and was instructed to go to the boat landing to catch a boat for the USS *Donner*.

At the boat landing I asked the petty officer in charge which ship was the *Donner*. He pointed to a gray ship about a mile offshore. She was a strange-looking ship with tall cranes. I had never seen anything like her before. I stood there gazing at her until the word came over the PA system that the boat from the *Donner* was at the landing. I grabbed my sea bag and boarded the boat. An officer and a second-class petty officer got on, too.

As the boat took off, they began to talk. I was looking at the *Donner*. I heard the officer ask the petty officer, "What kind of work does your girlfriend do?"

The petty officer replied, "She takes care of nigger babies."

My head snapped around, and I looked at them. They continued talking; I stared at them. Then I turned and faced the receding shore, thinking to myself, *Boy, you're in for it now.* I didn't look at the ship anymore until the boat engine slowed.

I went up the gangway, saluted the flag, and stepped onto the ship. I saluted the chief petty officer on duty, saying, "Adolph Newton, Motor Machinist's Mate Third Class, reporting for duty."

The chief saluted, took my orders, and read them to himself. He went over to the officer who had come over on the boat and said, "Sir, we have this colored boy here. What do you want to do with him?"

The officer replied, "Put him with the steward's mates."

The chief said, "Sir, he's not a steward's mate."

The officer said, "Call his division officer and find out what he wants to do with him."

The chief picked up the phone, dialed a number, and said, "We have a colored boy down here on the quarterdeck who is a motor machinist's mate third class. What do you want to do with him?" There was a pause, then he hung up the phone. He picked up the microphone and called, "Packard, Motor Machinist First Class, report to the quarterdeck."

The first class appeared. The chief introduced us, then said, "This man is assigned to the Engineering Division. Take him up there and find him a bunk."

Packard said, "OK. Come on."

We went through a hatch, down a passageway, and up a ladder into a large compartment where no fewer than sixty men slept. There were bunks three rows high.

Packard said, "Here you are." We were at a bottom bunk next to a hatch that led to the mess hall. He said, "It's almost chow time. Get your things, and I'll show you where to wash up."

We went through the mess hall. I noticed another mess hall next to it. We stepped into a passageway running starboard to port. The head was on the port side. Halfway there, we met a first-class boatswain's mate. This guy, like Packard, was over six feet tall, but whereas Packard was slim, this guy was big.

He said, "Hey, Packard, where are you going with this guy?"

Packard answered, "I'm taking him to the engineers' head so that he can wash up for chow."

The boatswain said, "Ain't no nigger going to use any head that my men clean up. My men don't clean up after no nigger, and he is not going to use it."

Packard said, "This man is assigned to the Engineering Division, and he is going to use the engineers' head."

The boatswain got right in Packard's face. He said, "This nigger is not going to use the engineers' head. Let him go down below where he belongs and use the steward's mates' head. My men do not clean up behind no nigger."

There were eight or nine guys with him, and since Packard and I had stopped in the middle of this passageway, we were now in the middle of seventy or eighty guys. There was not a friendly face among them. Packard said to me, "You'll have to wait till I get the engineering officer so we can get this thing straightened out."

Now, I thought I should go with Packard. Anything might happen to me there in the middle of all those guys. If one of those guys, especially the big boatswain, took a swing at me, I would be a fucked duck before Packard could get back with the engineering officer. All sorts of thoughts were racing through my mind. I leaned back against the bulkhead and watched the boatswain rave. I knew I didn't stand a snowball's chance in hell if I started anything. Something Wickline had said came to mind. I remembered him telling me, "You can't beat them all," and I totally agreed. I didn't say a word; I just stared at the boatswain. I couldn't hear everything he was saying; I was thinking about what to do until the doctor came.

The boatswain was still talking. "I don't know what the Navy is coming to, letting niggers in the Seaman-Fireman Branch. There's one thing you can be sure of: you will not use the engineers' head. You go down below and use the steward's mates' head. My men do not clean up after niggers."

I didn't say a word. It seemed as if Packard had been gone an hour, but I guess it was only about five or ten minutes before I heard a voice back in the passageway saying, "Make way."

I turned to see a lieutenant coming through the crowd with Packard. He came up to the boatswain and asked, "What's going on here?"

The boatswain said, "No nigger is going to use any head that my men have to clean up."

The lieutenant said, "This man is assigned to the Engineering Division, and he will sleep in the engineers' compartment. He will use the engineers' head, and there will be no more said about it."

The boatswain said, "If I have to associate with niggers, I'm going to get out of the Navy."

The lieutenant said, "Suit yourself. There will be no more said about it." He turned and walked away.

Packard told me, "Come on," and we started toward the head.

The boatswain was still in the way, so we just went around him and went into the head. The guys who were there when we entered all left. I washed up, and Packard and I went back to my bunk.

Packard said, "Come on, and I'll show you where the chow line is."

We went up a ladder and out on deck. We were now two decks above where I had boarded the ship. I got at the end of the chow line. Packard left. I had been on this ship for only an hour, and already I was ready to get off. Everyone who came up to the line got in front of someone already ahead of me; thirty minutes in line, and I was still last. Finally one guy got behind me, and the line started to move. I got my meal and went into the mess hall. I sat down at a table where there was an empty seat; the tables seated twelve. When I sat down, the fellows seated at the table got up. They either went into the next mess hall or found other seats at other tables.

Now I had the whole table to myself. In a way, this was all right; half the time in a military mess hall you're passing something up or down the table. I got everything that I needed, placed it in front of me, and ate my meal with no interruptions. Everyone was staring at me. There was a lot of murmuring; I couldn't hear the words. I finished my meal, took my tray to the scullery, and went back to my bunk.

When I went to chow there had been only one vacant bunk, the bottom one that had been assigned to me. On my return, there were six. I had my choice, but I took the bunk I had been assigned and made up my bed. I then decided to take a walk around the ship to check things out.

I came upon a steward's mate in a passageway. I said, "Hey man, how are you doing?"

He said, "OK."

I said, "Say, tell me something. Just what kind of ship is this?"

He asked, "Did you just come on board?"

"Yes. I'm in the Engineering Division."

"Yeah! You're the first Negro to come on board in that division," he told me.

"Yeah, I just found out."

He said, "We're serving the officers' chow now; I'll see you later. Our compartment is down that ladder. We all will be down there in a couple of hours."

I said, "OK," and he left.

I walked around out on deck. Everyone stared; as soon as I got near, they would turn their backs. I thought, *Lord, if this ain't a mess that I'm in.* I went back and sat on my bunk, thinking. I thought about what they had told us at Great Lakes ("You have to be better than good") and at Hampton ("You have to use your head"), and about what Wickline had told me ("You can't beat them all"). I thought about the guy at Treasure Island who had told me I would have to find some white guy I thought I could beat and kick his ass—that's what I would have to do to make them leave me alone. After some more thought, though, that didn't seem to be such a good idea. If the guy I picked got some help, I would really be in a jam. I had to put all these things together and make one hell of a decision. The only sure thing was that I had to use all the advice I had been given.

Packard came by and said he would show me around the ship in the morning. I went down to the steward's mates' compartment. Some of them were getting ready to go on liberty, and some were just lounging around. I asked, "Hey, can anybody tell me what kind of ship this is?"

One guy answered, "This is a landing ship dock—an amphibious ship."

I said, "Those boats I saw up on deck aren't amphibious boats."

He said, "No, those are officers' boats. When we're not on maneuvers, we follow the fleet and provide transportation for the officers and enlisted men."

This sounded good—following the fleet around. I asked, "How is the liberty in Norfolk? I was here a few years ago, and it was a hole."

Someone said, "It still is."

We talked for a couple of hours before I asked, "What time is taps?"

"Nine-thirty," a sleepy voice answered.

I said, "I guess I'll go up and get ready to hit the sack."

I went up to the engineers' compartment. I undressed, got my soap, towel, and a change of underwear, and went to the head to take a shower. There were a few guys in the shower; they left as soon as I came in. I had the whole shower pit to myself. That was all right with me; I always felt somewhat embarrassed showering with other guys.

I went back, got in my bunk, and tried to go to sleep, but I couldn't. There was a steady parade of crew members coming by to see if I was bunking in the engineers' compartment and where. I lay there watching them look at me. This went on until taps.

The word came over the PA system: "Lights out. The smoking lamp is out in all compartments. Silence about the decks."

The parade stopped, and I tried to go to sleep, thinking about a song I had heard by the "Wings over Jordan" choir called "Over My Head I See Trouble in the Air." Since I was the only occupant of these six bunks, I decided to move to the top bunk. There are often problems for a man in a lower bunk. When guys come in from liberty, they're in bad shape, and sometimes they step on the guy in the bottom bunk; they may throw up on him, and sometimes they urinate on him, thinking that they're in the head. You don't have these problems in the top bunk; you can sleep in peace.

The next morning when reveille sounded, I had to admit it was the loudest I'd ever heard; it would've waked the dead. I got my things together and went to the head. It was crowded, but everyone left as soon as I came in. I washed up; for some reason it took me longer than normal. I went back, put my things in my locker, made my bunk, folded the bunk out of the way, went to the mess hall, and got in the chow line. The performance of the previous day was repeated: everyone kept cutting into the line, and when I finally sat at a table, everyone got up. I ate and went back to my bunk.

I was arranging my locker when Packard came by and said, "We muster [assemble for roll call] on the five-inch gun deck at eight o'clock. You stay here. I'll come back for you, and we'll go up together."

I said, "OK."

He came back about quarter to eight, and we went up to the five-inch gun deck, which really was a five-inch gun placement, with a large open deck just in front of the bridge. The divisions started forming with the deck force on one side and the engineers on the other. The stewards and steward's mates formed on the end, between the deck force and the engineers, facing forward.

The enlisted man who had come back on the boat when I first came aboard came by. I asked Packard who he was and learned that he was the mailman. The officers were coming out. When I saw the same officer who had come on the boat, I asked about him, too. Packard said, "That's our executive officer. We call him Grasshopper."

I said, "Holy cow."

"What's wrong?" Packard asked.

"Nothing."

After muster, Packard showed me around. As we went through the ship we came upon a room with a nameplate that read "Injector-Blower-Pump Room." I asked if this room was being used; this was right down my alley, I told him, for I was an injector, blower, and pump specialist.

Packard said, "You are? That's great, but we don't use that room."

I asked, "What do you do with your old blowers, pumps, and injectors?"

"We throw them over the side."

I couldn't believe it. "Holy mackerel! That's kind of expensive, isn't it? Maybe there's something I could do. I'm a specialist on these things."

Packard said he would talk to the chief about it. We left the room and continued the tour, but I was thinking just how expensive this ship was. Here was a room designed for the overhaul of injectors, blowers, and pumps that wasn't used. They just threw those parts over the side when they overhauled an engine. I knew that injectors cost around $40, blowers more than $200, and pumps $50. Blowers were changed only when necessary during overhaul, but in the course of a year an engineer might use as many as twenty-four injectors for overhauling and tuning up a single engine. That was a lot of money being thrown into the ocean.

We went to a catwalk overlooking a large open area inside of the ship, called the well deck. I looked down into it on row after row of LCMs. There were at least twenty LCMs in that well deck, and in each one was a smaller landing craft called a PL (personnel, light). Packard said that the ship would ballast down to a certain depth in order to float all the boats in the well deck. The tailgate would be lowered, the boats would pull out, and cranes would take the PLs out of the LCMs. We then went up onto the mezzanine deck where the officers' boats were kept. These boats were covered. I learned that we carried everything from the full admiral's barge to the plain officers' boats. These boats and their crews were assigned in accordance with the rank of the officer requesting them.

Packard went on to explain that the engineers were somewhat green; for example, two of them had put an engine on the testing rack with a piston missing. I had seen that before, but on deck at muster I had noticed that most of the engineers were petty officers. I had to wonder where they got their ratings. We went to the engineers' office, where I met Lieutenant

Roper, the officer in charge of the Boat Engineers' Division. Packard gave me the number of a PL, which was the boat I would be responsible for.

I went down in the well deck and found my boat. I should have expected it to have a dead engine; it did. I would have to overhaul it. I nosed around the boat to find out just what I had to do. I knew one thing: it took two men to overhaul an engine effectively. I would have to find Packard and request a fireman to work with me on this overhaul job. Since it was near chow time, I decided to find him after lunch.

That afternoon I was down in the boat when a fireman showed up. The first thing he did was sit down. I asked, "Are you the fireman that is to help me with this overhaul?"

He said, "Yes."

I asked, "Do you know anything about these engines?"

He answered, "A little."

"Have you ever overhauled any of these engines?"

"No."

I said, "OK, when we get finished, you'll be able to do it yourself. It should take three or four days. It's too late to start today, so I'll show you what we're going to do tomorrow."

The next day, using a chainfall, we lifted the engine and placed it on two six-by-sixes in the boat and began to disassemble it until it was time to quit. Then the word came over the PA system: "Now hear this. Liberty will be until Monday at 0800 hours. At 1000 hours the ship will get under way for Izmir, Turkey. That is all."

The ship was going to get under way, and I didn't have a dollar to go ashore before we left because I had been in the brig in Washington last payday. *Now this is really a bitch,* I thought.

10 *Sailor, Again*

I went back up to the compartment. I washed up for chow and was lying on my bunk when a white guy came up to me and said, "Say, are you going ashore on your seventy-two-hour pass?"

I said, "No. I won't make this one because I missed the last pay."

He asked, "How much would it cost you to get home and back?"

"I don't know."

"Would $50 help?"

"It sure would."

He reached into his wallet and gave me $50.

I said, "Hey, thanks man." I was getting out of the bunk now. "What's your name? My name is Newton."

"Cummings," he answered.

"Thanks, Cummings, and I'll see you on payday."

He walked away. I called after him and asked how to get a bus to Baltimore. He said, "You would have to go over to Newport News to get the bus."

"How do you get to Newport News from here?"

"Go out the gate, turn right, and you'll be right at the Newport News ferry. When you get to Newport News, just ask anybody, and they'll tell you where the bus station is."

I thanked him again and got myself together, and off to Baltimore I went.

The weekend was nice, but uneventful. Before I knew it, I was heading back. On the bus back I thought about the ship; for some reason I liked this ship. I didn't care for the situation I was in, and there seemed to be a lot of people on board who didn't care for me, but I liked the ship. I would have guessed that there were three hundred men in the crew. So far Packard and Cummings were the only white crew members who had anything decent to say to me. The fireman who was helping me overhaul the engine only spoke when I said something to him, and then it was work-related. The situation was puzzling; I wasn't quite sure what I should do.

I got back to the ship late Sunday night. Shortly after Monday morning muster the word came over the PA system: "Set the special sea detail." That meant that we were preparing to get under way. A detail was sent out to release the anchor chain from the buoy; the captain's gig was hoisted aboard. There was a long blast of the ship's horn, and we steamed out of Hampton Roads for Izmir, Turkey, which I had never heard of before.

The fireman and I had finished overhauling our engine; it had taken four days. The day we put the engine on the testing stand, there must have been fifty guys from the shop standing around, and a group of officers on the deck above, watching. I wasn't worried about the engine starting, but all those people standing around made me nervous. *If this engine doesn't start,* I thought, *I might as well jump over the side; I'll be the laughingstock of the ship.*

Packard and the engineering chief petty officer were standing less than two feet away. I told Packard, "Don't worry, it's going to run." He smiled, but I knew that this was no joking matter.

Everyone could see that I was shaking, but I couldn't stop. I connected the battery and placed a screwdriver on the solenoid contacts. The engine turned over and smoked, which was normal for an engine that had just been overhauled. I held the governor wide open and hit the contacts again. The engine started. Packard was smiling for real now.

"OK?" I asked.

"OK," he said, and they left. The crowd of onlookers broke up. I was sure that some of them were disappointed, but I was happy. Now they knew what I had known all along: I knew my job, and I did good work.

The next day we put the engine in the boat and hooked it to the propeller shaft. We were ready to go; all we needed was a coxswain to run the boat.

Packard came up and told me that I'd better take a look at my battle station. I went to the board in our compartment, and my eyes almost popped out. I had just about every conceivable assignment. For general quarters, I was assigned to a repair group just above the port-side engine room. For fires, I was assigned to operate the main fire pump, which was below decks, in a room where you locked yourself in, put on headphones, and waited for orders from the bridge. For rescue, I was assigned the #1 rescue boat on the port side. If we had to abandon ship, I was assigned to a raft aft on the starboard side. For gas attack, I believe I had something to do—I forget what it was. I don't know how I got some of these assignments. For example, rescue boat duty is high priority. It's usually given to guys who brown-nose. The fire pump engine station carries the same status, and I got both within my first six days aboard.

The *Donner* was not one of the Navy's fastest ships. By Saturday we had not yet reached our first stop, the Rock of Gibraltar, where we were supposed to refuel. We had a captain's inspection scheduled for Saturday. I hadn't seen the captain of this ship and was curious to find out who he was.

For captain's inspection, everyone lined up in formation, in dress uniform (except those on watch). The captain inspected the ship, then the crew. The call came, "Attention," as he came on deck. The captain was a tall man, but something about him was curious. I had to think for a moment before I realized that he wore hard-heeled shoes. He was the first person in the Navy I had ever seen wear hard-heeled shoes. Whenever he walked on those steel decks, if we were down below we could hear that clink-clink sound and knew who was walking overhead.

The captain stopped in front of me and said, "You just came aboard."
I said, "Yes, sir."
He asked, "Don't you have any ribbons?"
"Yes, sir."
"The next time, I want to see them. You should be proud of your ribbons."
"Yes, sir."
He moved on.

I brought the ribbons as soon as I could; the ribbons I had been awarded were the American Theater Ribbon, the Asiatic Pacific Theater Ribbon, the

Victory Medal, the Navy Occupation Medal, and the Philippine Liberation Ribbon with one star.

The Rock of Gibraltar came into view the next day. Gibraltar was a fortress guarding the entrance to the Mediterranean Sea. It was said to be impregnable, though with these new atomic bombs, anything could be destroyed, it seemed. The fortress was manned by the British even though Gibraltar belonged to Spain. You could stand in Gibraltar and see Morocco, which was ten miles away. It had been a refueling point for ships for years. We could go onto Gibraltar but couldn't go ashore in Spain. Franco, the dictator who ruled Spain, would not let anyone into the country in a military uniform.

We tied up to a fueling pier, and the port side had liberty; I went ashore the next day. Gibraltar had plenty of bars and stores, but that was about all. We could sit around and watch the all-girl bands and girl dancers stomping their heels to some Spanish tunes that I didn't understand. That was it in Gibraltar. Nothing happened there, for it was watched by the British, who kept a tight rein on things. Spanish employees came to Gibraltar in the morning and had to return to Spain by eleven o'clock at night.

I had come ashore with some of the stewards. We went from club to club, looking at those girls stomping on the floor as if they were trying to break their ankles. We were hoping to see if there was something going on that the British Military Police had missed, but it was no use; they had everything sewed up tight.

We were in one of the clubs drinking when that first-class boatswain's mate Packard and I had had the run-in with walked in. At our table were a first-class steward named Mitchell, who was in charge of all the stewards and steward's mates on the ship; a second-class steward, also named Mitchell, who was really built and just a little shorter than the boatswain's mate; and Cass, the captain's steward, who was a second class.

I said, "Here comes that son of a bitch that started all that trouble when I came aboard." They all turned around to see who I was speaking about. No one said anything; they all knew him.

He sat at a table, then came over to me and said, "Are you talking about me?"

I said, "Did you hear me say anything about you?"

He said, "I want to know."

I said, "Get lost."

He looked at me, then went back to his table.

When we left that club it was time to go back to the ship. We were standing on the float waiting for the boat from the ship, and here came that boatswain's mate up to me again.

He said, "You're one of those smart niggers, aren't you?"

I said, "So what if I am, you bigheaded motherfucka? So what if I am?"

"I'll show you," he said, and he came at me.

One of the stewards named Mitchell—the second class, the guy who was really built—pushed him back and said, "Why don't you pick on someone your size?"

The boatswain said, "You are my size."

Mitchell hit him and laid him out on the float. A bunch of the white guys helped him up and told him to forget it. The boat came, and we all went back to the ship.

Later that night I was lying on my rack trying to go to sleep when that boatswain came by with some of his deck hands. He was hollering that he was going down to the stewards' compartment and "kill that nigger." He had to pass my bunk to reach the ladder to the stewards' compartment. When he got to me, he stopped and put his arm up on my rack, knowing that I was there. He had one of the longest folding knives I had ever seen. He moved his hand so that the knife touched my side. I was lying on my right side, on my right elbow, looking at him; he wasn't drunk. He was trying to get some of the engineers to go with him. They told him not to go down there because if he did, he wasn't going to come back in the same shape. After a while he went back to his compartment.

When I went to the stewards' compartment later, I told them what had happened. They said, "Let that big motherfucka come on down here; we got something for his big ass."

Just to be on the safe side, I asked, "Are there any empty racks down here?"

They said, "No, but there're plenty down in the troop compartment."

I said, "Troop compartment? You mean this thing carries troops, too?"

"Oh, yes, a whole lot of them." They opened an escape hatch in the deck, and we went down into the troop compartment. I was really surprised at what I saw. That ship could carry hundreds of troops. I didn't count the racks, but there were enough to triple the size of the crew and more. They were all made up, ready for use. Now I understood why the ship had a four-striper for a captain. I found a rack near the escape hatch and went to sleep, wondering what other surprises were on this ship. I also wondered why Packard hadn't showed me this when he was supposed to be showing me the ship.

The next night I was back in my rack in the engineers' compartment, and we were under way for Turkey.

On the way to Turkey we were briefed as to what we were to do and what not to do. We were on a mission called Show the Flag. The American Mediterranean Fleet was coming to Izmir, and the Turkish people would be brought aboard the various ships for tours. Of course, they would be amazed at the size of these ships. That would give the Turkish people confidence in America, plus the American crews would go ashore and spend a lot of money, which would help the Turkish economy; everybody would benefit. Boats would be assigned to ships according to their needs. One important caution: when we went ashore, we were not to consume any food or water; anything we drank had to be fermented or contain alcohol. Under no circumstances were we to have sexual relations with any of the women, for they all were suspected of having some form of venereal disease. Everyone laughed at this; that was like telling a bunch of kids not to eat any candy because it wasn't good for them. To put the icing on the cake, they gave each of us a map showing us the off-limits areas in Izmir.

We anchored a half-mile offshore and began to ballast down. The tailgate was lowered, and the LCMs were brought off. The water was crystal blue, so clear that you could see the rudder and propeller of the ship. The ships of the fleet came in and anchored—destroyers, cruisers, and an aircraft carrier.

My boat was sent to a destroyer. On our first trip I noticed that the distance from the water to the top of the landing area was only about eighteen inches. When I asked about this, I was told that the Mediterranean had no tide, and it flowed toward the Atlantic Ocean.

The next day I had liberty; I went ashore with some of the stewards and steward's mates. The first thing that greeted us was a sign saying "Welcome Blue Jakets"; they had spelled *jackets* wrong. We were told that this was the first time Americans had been here in more than twenty years, and only a few people spoke any English. Izmir was a very clean city; you didn't see trash in the streets, as was common in the States. It had wide streets and horse-drawn carriages for taxis. We hailed taxis and went to a bar. After a few drinks we decided that it was time to find the off-limits area. We got back into taxis and showed one of the drivers the map. He took us right to the place. We paid the drivers the way we always did whenever we didn't speak the language: we held out the money and let them take what they wanted.

Prostitution was legal in Turkey; the prostitutes in Izmir were inside a walled-in area. But when we got there we were confronted with a slight problem: there was a group of Shore Patrolmen at the entrance to the walled-in area. Then an Izmir policeman beckoned us to come with him. We followed him along the wall to where it was only about six feet high. He signaled for us to go over the wall, and we did.

There were a lot of large houses on the other side of this wall. We went into the first house. Girls were seated on a long bench; they all had on robes that came to the floor. I picked out a real light-brown-skinned girl with auburn hair. As she stood up, I noticed that there were heaters on the floor between their feet. I pointed the heaters out to the other guys. This was my first time in a legal house of prostitution, and I had never seen anything like it. We all went to separate rooms and took care of business. We met afterward and went back over the wall into the city.

We found a bar nearby, had a few drinks, then went back to the wall and over, to the same place; I picked out the same girl. That auburn-haired Turkish girl had a ring in my nose. I was supposed to be a tough guy with women. When I wanted them, I would get them. When I was finished, I would throw them away like a cigarette butt. This time was a little different. We never understood each other; I didn't know what she was saying, and she didn't know what I was saying, but I couldn't get enough.

We went back to the bar, had a few more, then back to the wall, tried it again, only this time when I went over the wall I landed in a knee-deep pit of lime. Picture a sailor in his dress blue uniform, except everything from his knees down is pure white. I couldn't go into that house looking like this, so I told the guys I would see them back at the ship. Everyone I met laughed at me; I had to laugh at myself, but I'd had a nice time. I had to throw the pants and socks away but ended up with an extra pair of work shoes.

The fleet pulled out the next day, and we returned to Norfolk.

The white guys on the ship had started to shove me around. They were bumping into me when there was no need for contact. That sailor at Treasure Island had warned me that this would happen. The time had come for me to do something. I had to look over the crew and find a guy to beat, and I had to do it soon. I saw no way that a fight could be avoided; better to do it my way than let them have it their way.

In the meantime, I went on liberty in Norfolk with a couple of the stewards. They showed me how to get around there. Norfolk was the worst hole in the world; segregation started as soon as you stepped outside the base gate. When you got on a streetcar, all Negroes had to move to the rear. There was a yellow line painted on the floor in the rear; Negroes had to stay behind that line. There were maps all over Norfolk showing the area for the Negroes and the area for the whites. Negroes had to stay inside the area marked with a red circle; everything outside the circle was for whites. The main street in Norfolk for Negroes was Church Street—the filthiest street I have ever been on. The street was made of cobblestones. The stores there had meat hanging out on the street; the flies were having a holiday on meat that people were supposed to eat. In hot or warm weather, or after a rain, the place stank to high heaven. You could walk down the street with your eyes closed and tell what you were passing—a bar, a meat store, or a woman—just by the smell.

To add insult to injury, the Norfolk police seemed to have a hobby of locking up sailors; it was as if they had a quota of sailors to arrest each night. All over town it was said that sailors were no good, and no decent girl in Norfolk would be seen with one. I believed this; there had to be girls in Norfolk other than the whores who walked Church Street, but I never saw them. The bars on Church Street were holes in the wall. There was only one I could call a nice place, a bar called Russell's. The owner didn't allow any solicitation in his bar; that cut out a lot of his business—sailors and whores. This became my hangout.

By now I had picked out the guy on the ship I was going to fight; all I had to do was wait for the right time. It was not a long wait.

One day when the guys were all in the compartment, I saw him coming through the hatch near me. I started through the hatch, too. We bumped, for only one person could get through at a time. I said real loud, "Motherfucka, didn't I tell you about fucking with me?" and hit him. We tangled, but I had the upper hand. Some of the guys soon broke it up, and I argued with the guy for a while, but nothing else happened. I went over to my bunk and sat down, waiting; if anything was going to happen, it would be now. I slept with a smile on my face that night, thanks to the guy at Treasure Island.

I started to make a few friends. One of the white engineers came up to me on deck one day and said, "I would like to be your friend, but I have to stick with the other guys; so don't talk to me when they're around. And remember, even if you're right, you're wrong if they say you are, and I'm going along with them."

I said, "All right, I won't get you in any trouble." I figured that even this half-effort was better than nothing at this stage of the game. At least I knew this guy wasn't totally against me.

Another time a guy came up to me and said, "We don't all dislike you, but this is something new for us."

I said, "I'm beginning to find that out, thanks."

He walked away. I thought, *What in the hell am I going to do now?*

An announcement came over the PA system that we were going to get under way for the naval base at Guantánamo Bay, Cuba. A cruiser left New York the same time we left Norfolk and reached Guantánamo Bay a day before we did.

On this trip I learned that the water around Cuba had so much salt in it that we couldn't evaporate it to make fresh water. As a result, we had to conserve water. Shower period was limited to ninety minutes; that was the end of having the shower to myself. Still, it was a relief to leave the cold weather of Norfolk and enter the warm climate of the Caribbean Sea.

The naval base at Guantánamo Bay (called Gitmo by sailors) is tucked away on the southeastern tip of Cuba. I got angry as soon as I set foot on the base; it seemed as if every sailor on the base had a Negro girl making his bed. I went into three or four dorms and saw the same thing: each dorm had about thirty beds and about twenty-five girls. How could the Navy allow this? We didn't have this good a deal in the Philippines.

The guys on the ship said that in Havana, the capital of Cuba, there were topless barmaids. I had never heard of such a thing, and I did want to see them, but Havana was a long way from Gitmo Bay. They said that Cuba was America's whorehouse, and I didn't see anything on the base to give me a reason to disagree. The main item they sold on the naval base was women's purses made of alligator skin; some had a whole baby alligator on them. Perfume and jewelry were the other big sellers. I was glad to leave Gitmo Bay.

We returned to Norfolk in time for Christmas. After the holidays we got a new captain and executive officer. The captain was a full commander and a submariner; the executive officer was a lieutenant commander. A couple of days after the change of command, "Newton, Engineman Third Class, report to the five-inch gun deck for captains' mast" came over the PA system. What the hell had I done now?

I was working on my boat and had to wash up and get into my undress blues before I reported. The ship's yeoman was waiting for me. When he saw me he went into the captain's quarters; a couple of minutes later he came out and told me to come in. When I went in, I was shocked to see every officer on the ship already there. What the hell was this? I had been to captain's mast quite a few times, but this took the cake. Because I had the utmost respect for officers, I became frightened. I had no idea what had happened or was about to happen.

The captain spoke.

"Newton, I am the new commanding officer of the USS *Donner,* and I want to take this opportunity to welcome you aboard."

It was as if a five-hundred-pound weight had been lifted off my shoulders. I crumbled inside.

The captain continued. "I understand that you are the only Negro on board in the Seaman-Fireman Branch. I want you to be a credit to your race."

I struggled to answer. "Yes, sir."

He went on. "I also want you to know that discrimination will not be tolerated aboard the *Donner.* What are you smiling about?"

I said, "Nothing, sir," thinking that if he had about five hours I could tell him all about discrimination on the *Donner.* Then we would take a break.

The captain went on. "I also want you to know that if at any time you feel that you have a problem, you can come to my quarters without asking permission from any of these officers, and we'll get to the bottom of it. Is that clear?"

I said, "Yes, sir."

The captain said, "That is all."

"Thank you, sir." I saluted, did an about-face, and walked out, thinking that it wouldn't be long before I had to take him up on that offer to talk.

I was amazed by this experience. All of the captain's masts I'd had previously had been for punishment; I had thought that was all they were for.

Maybe I was making some progress. Maybe now someone would listen to my complaints.

Things gradually began to change. I was assigned another boat, an LCM. I had been anticipating this for a while; I had wanted another engine to work on. To my surprise, this boat didn't need overhaul work, just some adjustments to the engines. By now the captain's cook and I had become good friends. When we came off liberty we would go up into the captain's pantry for a sandwich and coffee. As soon as the officers found out, though, the executive officer informed me that Officers' Country was out of bounds to me.

One payday one of the white guys I occasionally talked to called me aside. "Newton, there's a crap game down in the bilge. Why don't you come on down?"

I said, "Show me the way."

Lady Luck was with me, because I won big that day. And it was after that crap game that things for some reason began to change. People stopped leaving the head when I entered; guys stayed at tables in the mess hall when I sat down; a lot more of the guys talked to me. Three white guys moved back into the jackstay that I was in, and in a short period of time I was on speaking terms with most of the engineers and some of the deck force. I tried to figure out what had caused these changes but couldn't come up with an answer. Maybe there wasn't any one particular reason; most likely it was a combination of things. But from that day on there were only three guys on the ship who ever had money, and I was one of them.

Another Negro was assigned to the Engineering Division around this time; he came aboard one night. When Packard brought him into the compartment, he started yelling about his rights as a second-class engineman. I was lying on my bunk; he was given the bunk under me.

I said, "Hi," and he answered. Then he turned back to Packard and resumed his tirade.

"I don't have to lash my bunk bottom. I know my rights; I'm a second-class petty officer in the United States Navy."

"I'll take care of it," I said, jumping down off my bunk. I didn't know what Packard was thinking, but I could sense trouble. I knew that none of these white boys was going to lash up his bunk bottom.

Packard said to the new guy, "Come on. I'll get you some chow while he's doing that."

I went to the locker, got out a bunk bottom and some line, and lashed the bottom. This situation started me to thinking. I knew there were certain rights and privileges with each petty officer rate, but I never knew exactly what they were. I had never read what they were; I had never been in any situation to use them. I knew for certain that if I had not been a petty officer when I came on board this ship, I would have had many more problems than I did. This guy was going to have to use all his rights to keep the white guys off him. I believed he was right about not having to lash up his bunk bottom, and Packard knew it.

When the new guy returned, I was back in my bunk. He looked at his bunk. "Good, Bunky, good," he said.

We shook hands and introduced ourselves; he was from New York City. We had a brief conversation. As he talked he began to remind me of the guy at Treasure Island. He seemed to hate the world and everyone in it, especially white people. His voice had an acid tone whenever he talked about whites. This might have been what got him transferred to another ship five months later.

The next morning we got under way for Newport, Rhode Island. The ship was going to Newport to pick up some automobiles belonging to servicemen overseas. From Newport the ship would proceed to Naples, Italy, where we were to unload the cars. Then we were going to Piraeus, Greece, for two days. The next stop would be Beirut, Lebanon, where the Mediterranean Fleet would show the flag and we would provide services to the fleet.

When we left Newport, I had my first experience with a North Atlantic storm. The northern part of the Atlantic Ocean was known for its storms and rough water. This was no exception; we got lost for two days. The men on the bridge finally got the situation under control, and we were back on course.

When we were only a few hours out of Naples, the ship got into the sanitation stream coming out of the city. Everyone on deck was yelling; I went up to see what was going on. Everyone was looking over the side and pointing. I looked too, and to my surprise there were hundreds of rubbers floating on the water.

Someone hollered, "This is the place to be!"

Another guy said, "Everyone in this town must be getting some."

I had always thought that Catholics were bareback riders, and I said so.

Someone said, "Oh, yeah? What's that?" pointing to the water.

A strange thing about Naples was that there were no sea gulls flying around the ship. Sea gulls were usually the first things you saw; they let you know you were nearing land. Someone said the people here ate them—they ate dogs and horses, too. That was the situation in Italy just after the war.

I was standing on the deck with Cummings and three other white guys—Jones, Pot, and Slim; we were watching the cars from the ship being unloaded. It was dark, and since there were no lights on the pier, we were using floodlights from the ship. Someone got the idea that if we went down as part of the work detail and moved to the edge of the lights, we could slip into the darkness and go into town. We could get back before they finished unloading.

We ran back to our lockers to get money and took off. We had no idea where to go, but a little Italian boy came up to us. "Joe, you want to find some girls?" Everyone said yes. He said, "Come with me."

We followed this boy, who could not have been more than nine. He took us away from the waterfront, into town, but not far from the ship. There were houses with those balconies that go from one side of the street to the other, like those pictures you've seen of Italy. It was so dark, we had to use matches to find our way. There was a green slime on the balcony walls. I believe that Caesar himself must have pissed on those walls; the smell was so strong, it could have been there that long.

We went into an apartment. The boy was talking to three girls in Italian; we had no idea what he was saying. One girl left and returned with two more girls. The boy got into an argument with the girls; they seemed afraid of him. They all gave him money, and he started to leave.

Cummings said, "We'll want you to take us back to the waterfront."

He said, "OK," and sat in a chair to wait.

On the way back he took us a different way. We heard a lot of noise, like a stadium full of kids hollering at the same time. Someone asked what the noise was. The boy pointed to three barrack ships tied to the sea wall. He said that homeless children lived on those ships. There must have been thousands of them. I remember thinking that when they grew up, Italy was going to have something on its hands.

When we got back to the ship, we slipped back into the work party and went on board. The ship moved out to a fueling pier.

The next evening some Italians came out to the ship in boats, selling all kinds of things. About seven that evening word got around that ten Italian girls were aboard, and the price was a dollar or a pack of cigarettes. I went to my locker for money and cigarettes. We later found out that an Italian guy had brought ten daredevil girls out to the ship and got some of the crew interested. The crewmen helped them sneak aboard, using the permanent ladder on the fantail. Girls were in the boats in the well deck, up on the mezzanine deck in the officers' boats, and in the gear lockers on deck.

As I was waiting in my third line, the PA system crackled: "Set the special sea detail."

Everybody panicked. There were ten girls on the ship, and we were getting under way! There was more confusion than I had ever seen on a ship, worse than when the ship in the Philippines got torpedoed. About 70 percent of the crew were running; some were running forward, some were running aft. They were running up ladders, jumping down ladders, and jumping from boat to boat in the well deck. The girls were damn near on their own. They were trying to carry all those cigarettes, and hardly anyone was helping them. We were under way by the time they got the last girl off the ship.

Every man got into his rack and just lay there, panting.

The next morning everyone not on duty was at muster on the five-inch gun deck. The captain addressed us: "It is my understanding that there were some women on this ship last night, and one is still aboard."

Everyone looked around.

The captain instructed the division officer to hold a roll call and account for every man. The officers would then search every inch of the ship, he said, and the crew would remain at quarters until the search was completed.

The search took a few hours. No girl was found.

The captain had us muster again. "If any of you knows where this girl is, bring her to the wardroom immediately. Anyone caught with this girl after thirty minutes will be court-martialed. That is all."

We were dismissed, but no girl surfaced. The guys started to play jokes—at least I thought they were jokes. At chow time a guy would leave the mess hall with a tray of food. Everyone saw it, but no one followed to find out where he took it. No one wanted to be near this girl, if she was aboard, for fear of a court-martial.

One day after evening chow some guys came up to me and told me that the girl was hiding on my fire station.

I said, "What?"

None of these guys was smiling.

I said, "You guys ought to stop that shit." I walked away, but I hauled ass down to my fire station. I didn't see a girl, but there were cigarette butts with lipstick on the deck. I put them in my pocket, thinking that I was going to be court-martialed sure as hell. I didn't sleep at all that night.

To top this off, some guy was going around the night before we docked at Piraeus, taking up a collection to get the girl back to Italy. He must have collected hundreds of dollars, and no one questioned him. No one said anything about it.

This incident led to many conversations about the possibility of smuggling a girl onto a ship. We all agreed that it wouldn't be hard. None of us had heard of it being done successfully; there were lots of stories about the failures. A group of five of us planned how we would bring a girl on board a ship tied to a pier in Norfolk. First, she would have to be a normal size, with no outstanding features. She would have to cut her hair. We would get her measurements and buy her a sailor's uniform, complete with shoes and hat. Getting her through the naval base gate wouldn't be a problem. Any sailor could tell you that security at any base was lax. All you did was hold up your ID card and walk in; no one ever checked it. When the streetcar stopped in front of the gate and fifty or sixty sailors got off and went through, no one checked them. Getting an ID card and a liberty pass for the girl wouldn't be difficult. Once she got to the ship, we would go up the gangway, drop our liberty passes into the box, and step through the hatch. No one would be suspicious at seeing a strange face; with a large crew, no one knew everyone in his division. Once she got through the hatch, it would be all over. She could stay in the troop compartment. She would not be alone.

When we arrived in Piraeus, Greece was in the middle of a civil war. There was no danger to us; we were on the good side of both of the groups that were fighting. This didn't sound very promising, but we went ashore anyway. There were trucks at the dock to take us to Athens. The trucks had to keep pulling off the road to go around shell craters. There were craters all over the area; they must have had a pretty good battle around there.

There isn't much I can say about Athens because it was dark when we arrived. Six or seven stewards and steward's mates and I were standing on a corner trying to figure out where to go. One of the steward's mates was a guy named Snake; he was uglier than the worst-looking guy you have ever seen. Another guy from the ship was coming up the street with a Greek girl. When she saw Snake, she screamed and ran. That prompted Cass, Mitchell, and me to leave the other guys; we couldn't have Snake scaring the women away.

We came to a bar and went in, looking for some women. There were no women there, but a group of British soldiers were drinking. We sat down and ordered a bottle of champagne. After we had paid for it, the British soldiers told us that the man who had waited on us had cheated us. The man got into an argument with them. The soldiers told us to let them order our next bottle. We did, and another argument started. We drank quickly and left before a fight started.

We finally found some girls because Cass could speak French; in almost all the ports we went to, the people understood French. After some more drinks we returned to where the trucks were waiting and went back to the *Donner.*

Early the next morning I was on deck, looking at a building atop a cliff or hill. I couldn't stop looking at it; I would go below and come back up to look at it again and again. It would be different colors at different times of the day. In early morning it would be pinkish; later it would be golden, around noon white, then golden and pinkish again in the evening. I never thought that I would spend a day going up and down ladders to look at some building. Later I found out that the building was the Parthenon.

The next day we left for Lebanon.

On the trip to Lebanon, Bob, one of the white guys in my division, asked me to come down to the tool crib where the guys gathered to shoot the shit before turning in. I had been aware of these gatherings for some time, but no one had ever asked me to join them, and I wasn't going to barge in on my own. There were five or six guys drinking coffee; they became silent when Bob and I came in. Bob went to a bucket of coffee cups soaking in water. He took a cup and started to pour his coffee.

As he poured, he said, "Come on, Newton, and get a cup of joe."

I said, "All right," and I poured myself a cup.

The guys were staring, and I knew it, but I decided to find out what, if anything, they were going to do.

One of them said, "Hey, Newton, I bet you were scared shitless when those guys told you there was a girl on your fire station."

"You guys had a good laugh about that, but I want you to know that I really *did* think somebody had stashed her there. If she had been there, she was going to get her ass out, and I didn't give a damn where she went. She wasn't staying on my fire station," I answered.

Somebody else said, "Aw, come on. You don't have to get mad about it."

I said, "It wasn't funny to me, and I'm telling all of you I didn't like it, so forget it."

Someone said, "Aw, come on, Newt, and sing us a song. All you colored people can sing."

Another guy said, "Yeah, sing 'Trees.' All coloreds know 'Trees.'"

I raised my voice a little. "Well, I will tell you something. You are looking at a Negro who cannot sing, and a Negro who also doesn't know 'Trees.'"

Someone asked, "Can you dance?"

"I'll see you guys later," I said as I left. As I walked back to my bunk I was humming 'Trees,' but I really cannot sing.

Lebanon is an Arab country bordering on the Mediterranean Sea. We arrived in Beirut about an hour before the fleet and began to ballast down. The incoming fleet consisted of destroyers, cruisers, and an aircraft carrier; this show of the flag would last for four days.

We followed the fleet around because warships could no longer carry boats; that practice had ended during the war. Warships carried only life rafts now and were too big to dock at many ports, so we furnished the boats that served as transportation between the ships and shore. Our boats weren't assigned to specific ships while in Beirut; there were more than enough crews to go around, so our duty was pretty light. We hauled civilians out to the ships and brought sailors to shore. The ships were open to visitors from 10 A.M. to 4 P.M.; liberty for the sailors lasted until midnight.

We got the usual lecture coming into Beirut, except that they also told us not to pay any attention to women walking arm in arm. They were not queer by any means; it was a custom. They told us not to travel alone, not to drink the water, and not to have relations with any of the women. Everybody groaned. They gave us maps of the area.

Beirut was a very clean and busy city. There was an abundance of cafés, bars, and nightclubs. Beirut had some of the best clubs I had ever seen. One in particular had a row of tables around the stage; behind that was another row on a higher level, and the rows kept going up. I was on about the fifteenth level with Cass and Mitch. We didn't understand the language, but we did enjoy the show. I told them I would like to build a club like that in the States.

After a while I left them and went on the back streets. I ran across a little Arab boy who couldn't speak English. I couldn't speak his language either, but I thought he was begging, so I gave him a handful of American money. I only hoped he was going home as he ran off.

Beirut had a lot of dark-skinned people. They, like the other foreign colored people I had met, didn't like to be called Negro; that term was strictly American. I didn't have any relations with a colored girl while I was in Beirut. At least I don't think I did; it was hard to tell, for almost everyone there was some shade of brown in skin complexion. A lot of the white guys from the ship had real dark girls; I heard them talking about it on the boat going back to the ship.

The next day I was down in the well deck checking out my boat when the call came over the PA system: "Newton, A. W., Engineman Third Class, man the captain's gig."

What? I wasn't the captain's engineer. I didn't mind being in on what was going on, but on board this ship it seemed like I was in on *everything*.

I ran to my locker and grabbed my soap and towel, then ran to the head and washed up, then back to my locker to change into my undress blues, then up on deck and out onto the boat boom and down the rope ladder to the captain's gig. I started the engine. Everything was ready. Now I could catch my breath.

The captain's coxswain came down. He was a third-class petty officer. He was an Indian; the guys on the ship called him anything they wanted, and he just smiled and said nothing. He spoke to me, and I said, "Hi. What in the hell is going on?" He said that the captain had let his engineer off that day. We took the boat around to the gangway to wait for the captain.

The captain and his guest came aboard, and we headed for shore. As we approached the landing, I noticed the coxswain having trouble with the controls. I went forward to find out what was wrong. He couldn't turn the throttle. I tried, and I couldn't, either. He had to turn the boat away from the landing. I got some tools and disconnected the throttle linkage to the governor of the engine and controlled the engine by hand. The captain was mad; he was red as a beet. I turned my attention back to the coxswain. Like most engineers, I could run these boats as well as a coxswain. Working together, we got the boat to the dock, but the trip was neither pretty nor smooth.

As soon as the captain and his guest went ashore, I tried to find out why the throttle had stuck. I checked the throttle linkage up to the control cabinet, and I found a can of metal polish wedged in the controls. I put everything back together, and we returned to the *Donner*. The captain came back on the crew's liberty boat, since he knew there was a problem with his own boat. As soon as he returned, he sent for me.

When I got to his quarters he asked me, "What happened to my boat?"

I answered, "Sir, a can of brass polish was wedged between the throttle and the control cabinet; it made us unable to turn the throttle."

He said, "How did the metal polish get there?"

"I don't know, sir; it was my first time on your boat."

The captain said, "OK, Newton, that is all."

The next day Bob, Pot, Jones, and I went ashore. We had a nice time, drinking and visiting the red-light district. It was on this liberty that Pot confessed his love for colored women.

Bob said, "It doesn't matter what color she is, as long as it's a woman."

Jones said color didn't bother him.

I said, "Well, fellows, it doesn't bother me, either. They most certainly have something for all of us."

On the way back to the ship that night we were talking when the guy called Slim hollered out, "Hey, Bob, bring your nigger-loving ass over here."

Everyone started shouting, "Shut up your hillbilly mouth."

He said, "Aw, I didn't mean nothing."

Someone said, "Shut up. You know Newton is standing there; just shut up."

The boat was silent for the rest of the trip to the ship. I was thinking that every time I was out with white guys, somewhere down the line these racial slurs came up, and the guy who said them was always drunk. I got the idea that if I wanted to know what these white guys really thought, all I had to do was go have a few drinks with them and wait; whatever attitudes were in them were going to come out.

The next day the fleet left Lebanon. We set course for Gibraltar; I'm not sure where the fleet went. We docked in Gibraltar for refueling; the crew had liberty.

I went ashore with the chief petty officer of the Engineering Division. We spent the evening strolling from bar to bar; it was a change from the shipboard routine. It was well after dark when we decided to return to the *Donner*. We came to the gangway leading down to the float where we caught the boat. The disbursing officer from the ship was at the top of the gangway. We saluted and spoke to him as we passed.

He said, "Hey, Chief. There's something down at the end of the pier that you might like."

The chief and I turned around and started down the pier.

The officer said to me, "Not you. You go back to the ship."

I said, "Why do I have to go back to the ship? The chief and I have been together all day."

He said, "I don't care. You go back to the ship."

I saluted him and said, "Yes, sir." I saluted again and said, "Anything you say, sir." I saluted once more, saying, "Yes, sir."

As I turned to go down the gangway, I noticed another chief standing nearby; it was the chief storekeeper. I went down the gangway and stood talking to some of the guys on the float. This chief storekeeper came up to me and said, "You can't talk to that officer like that."

I asked, "What did I say to the officer?"

He said, "You can't do what you did, saluting him like that."

I said, "There's nothing wrong with what I did; and you don't know what he did."

"I don't give a damn what he did. You can't do that."

"So what?"

"I'll show you what." He took off his coat and was coming at me. I was ready for him.

The disbursing officer stepped between us, saying, "All right, break it up."

I went over to the side of the float with some guys who wanted to know what was going on, and we waited for the boat. The boat came, and we all went back to the ship.

The next day we got under way for Norfolk. I was down in the well deck working on my boat when I was called to the five-inch gun deck for captain's mast. I thought, *They should just go on and assign me to the five-inch gun deck. I'm up there all the time, anyhow.*

When I reported, I saw the captain, the disbursing officer, the engineering officer of my division, the chief storekeeper, and the ship's yeoman. There was no doubt in my mind what this captain's mast was about.

The captain asked, "What happened with you and the disbursing officer last night?"

I said, "Nothing, sir. Chief Turpin and I were returning from liberty. The disbursing officer told the chief that there was something down at the end of the pier that he might like. The chief and I started down the pier, and the disbursing officer told me to go back to the ship. I tried to explain that the chief and I had been ashore together all day, so why did I have go back to the ship? The officer told me, 'Go back to the ship.' I saluted and went down to the gangway to the float."

The captain said, "About this saluting. It appears that you were saluting a little bit excessively. I can't find anything wrong with this, but I don't want to hear of it again."

I said, "Yes, sir."

The captain went on: "Now, what happened between you and the chief storekeeper?"

I said, "I was down on the float, and the chief storekeeper came down on the float and took his coat off and said that he was going to whip my ass."

The captain said, "Wait a minute. Did you say that this chief took his coat off?"

"Yes, sir," I replied.

The captain turned to the disbursing officer. "Did this chief have his coat off?"

The disbursing officer said, "Yes, sir."

The captain got mad. He turned to the chief and said, "Don't you know better than to take your coat off?"

Before the chief could answer, the captain said to me, "That is all, Newton."

I said, "Yes, sir," saluted, and walked out. I don't know what happened after I left, but something was telling me to be careful, and that song "Over My Head I See Trouble in the Air" stayed in my mind.

On our way back to Norfolk I went down to the tool crib several times. The conversation was about women almost every time. We never tired of talking about women; I guess it was a subject we all could talk on, for women were the same, no matter what color.

One day someone had the idea that we should have coffee cups with our names on them. I didn't resent this; I was ready to suggest the same thing, especially after hearing what some of these guys said they did on shore.

I would tell them lies about my relatives in Virginia who lived in a place called Useta. Its real name was Long Green, I said, but my relatives moved in and cut down all the trees; that's when they started to call it Useta. I would tell them about my uncles and aunt. One of my uncles was called Uncle Rip; he looked like he had been ripped out of a piece of paper. My other uncle was called Reared Her; they caught him in the barn one day doing it to a cow, and after that they always called him Reared Her. My Aunt Safronia did all the cooking, and she had her own marijuana patch. She stayed high all day. They owned a mule called Sitash; they were too religious to call the mule Shitass. Sitash would get into Safronia's marijuana patch and then would pull that plow all day; the sun would be going down, and old Sitash would be still plowing.

I would go on and on. They would be cracking up laughing. Of course, there is no such place as Useta, Virginia, but I do believe they thought it was true.

One night one of the guys changed the subject and said to me, "You coloreds are starting trouble. I don't know why you're rocking the boat."

I told him, "I don't believe in rocking the boat. I believe, turn the motherfucka over; let's all swim."

He went on just as if I had never said anything. "When I left down South," he said, "all the coloreds were happy. All you could hear was them singing."

I said, "Just the fact that you hear a Negro singing doesn't mean that he's happy. Do you think the slaves who had to pick cotton all day in the hot sun were happy when they were singing in the cotton fields? Of course not. What you didn't hear was what they were really singing about. I think the song 'Old Man River' tells the whole story: 'Tired of living, but scared of dying.' You're listening to the music and have no idea what they are singing *about*. When you go back home, you'd better listen to the words, for they might be singing about you."

We all had a good laugh.

Another of the Southern boys said, "You know, down where I come from you're not a man till you've had a colored woman."

I said, "And a whole lot of you are not a man *after* you've had one."

Another guy said, "Yeah, that's the trouble with the colored women; they're too free."

I was mad now. I said to him, "Tell me one reason why a Negro woman should be virtuous in the South. As soon as you white guys find out that she's a virgin, you're going to rape her. This is going on in the South right now."

"Oh, no, we don't," he said. "We don't do anything like that where I come from."

"Go jump in a lake," I said, and I left.

11 *Norfolk*

I was going on liberty. I boarded the streetcar just outside the gate.

In Virginia all Negroes had to go to the back of the streetcar. There was a line drawn on the floor of all public transportation, and all Negroes had to be behind that line. If there were whites standing and there were empty seats behind the line, the Negroes had to get up and move further back. If all the seats in the back had been taken (some by whites) and more Negroes got on, they would have to stand.

I was making my way to the rear of the streetcar when Pot jumped up. "Hey, Newt!" he called. "Come on and sit down here with Bob."

I sat down next to Bob; we started talking like nothing was going on. The streetcar was loaded mostly with sailors, so there was no problem. After a few blocks the conductor stopped the streetcar and came back to where I was seated and told me I had to go back behind that line. I got up and went behind the line, sat down, and started thinking. Here we were, Negro and white servicemen. We had all taken the same oath to lay down our lives for this country. On the ship we were part of a team, but when that team came ashore in the South, we had to split up. A lot of the guys on board the *Donner* had voiced their opinions against discrimination, but there was nothing we could do; it was a way of life.

We came into downtown Norfolk, where the whites got off. I had to go further, to transfer to another streetcar to get to Church Street. Pot and Bob came by me, on their way to the rear door, and said, "Come on, Newt, get off here."

I looked at them; I knew what was going to happen, but I got off the streetcar anyway. They had decided to take me into one of those white clubs to drink.

The three of us went into some bar in downtown Norfolk. I had long straight hair and brown skin, so I was going to try to pass as an Indian or Mexican. They ordered beer; the bartender brought it. I started drinking. Bob and Pot were talking; I remained silent. As luck would have it, Pot said something to me, and I answered him. The bartender was nearby and heard my voice. He told me to lean over the bar. He whispered into my ear to get out as soon as I finished that beer. I told Bob and Pot what the bartender had said, and we left.

When we got outside I told Bob and Pot to come with me up into the colored section, because no one would bother us there. We got a cab and went up to Church Street. We went into a little club and drank beer. We had been talking for a long time when three Shore Patrolmen came in. One of them was white; the other two were Negroes. The white one started toward us. He stopped in front of our table and said, pointing to Bob and Pot, "You two are out of bounds, and you are to get out of this district now."

We left. I told them of another bar, across town; no one would bother us there. We got a cab and went to the other bar. It had live entertainment, and we were enjoying ourselves when the same three Shore Patrolmen came in. This time all three came over to our table. The white one said, "I told you two guys to get out of this district. If I see you in this district again, I'm going to lock you up."

I told Bob and Pot to go on, and I would see them back at the ship. They left.

I sat in the club for a while, thinking. I tried to figure out how in the hell I had gotten on board the *Donner*. I was convinced that it was not a coincidence that I had been sent to a ship that had no other Negroes in the Sea-man-Fireman Branch. Not that I didn't like the *Donner,* because I did; it was a challenge, and I liked that. Some things about the ship seemed to be improving. Whenever I met any of these white guys downtown, they would come up to me and speak. If they had their wives or girlfriends with them, they would introduce us. This made me feel accepted as a crew member and a friend. But because of some stupid law, we had to go separate ways.

One evening in the steward's mates' compartment we were listening to some jazz records. At the same time, the mailman was up in the radio shack playing those eternally boring hillbilly records over the PA system. Every day, all day, all night, he played hillbilly records. Not only the Negroes, but also a lot of the whites objected to hearing this music all the time. I said to one of the steward's mates, "Give me some of these records." I went to the radio shack and asked the mailman if I could play some jazz. He agreed to let me play them; for an hour a day I would play jazz.

The officers and crew members enjoyed the music. At their suggestion I got money from the ship's fund and bought more records. There was a new music, called bebop, coming out. When I bought records, I would buy both the melody version and the bebop version of the same song, if it was available, and I would play both to show the difference between the two. I really never knew just what bebop was, except it was a totally new pre-sentation of jazz. Even the guys who created bebop didn't know exactly what it was. I heard them refer to it as "Freedom of Expression," "Flatted Fifths," or "G-sevens." If the creators of the music weren't sure, I certainly wasn't, but it was a new sound that people liked, and I had a lot of fun play-ing it.

One day I only had a few dollars, and I went into Norfolk. I was sitting in a bar, and my steady girl walked in. I asked her for some on the cuff.

"Newton," she said, "I would, but I would be looking up at you and you don't have nothing, and you would be looking down at me and I don't have anything, so wait till one of us has something."

I told her, "I know who that one is!"

One night while we were asleep, there was a boom. Everyone woke up and hit the deck asking what it was. At 2 A.M. the whole compartment was ordered to muster on the five-inch gun deck. The Engineering Division warrant officer wanted to know who in the compartment had thrown a fire-cracker at the officer of the day. Nobody said anything.

He said, "You'll all stay here until I find out who did it. Stand up like white men."

I said, "Just a minute. I'm standing here. I am not white, and I did not do it."

"I threw the firecracker," Bob said.

The warrant officer told the rest of us to go to bed.

The next day I was ordered to report to the engineers' office. The warrant officer was there, alone. He got up and locked the door; I thought he wanted to fight.

He said, "What did you mean, calling me down in front of the men?"

I said, "What did you mean, saying what you said?"

"I don't want it to happen again," he said.

"I don't want it to happen again, either," I answered.

He said, "That is all."

I went back to work.

A rumor was circulating that the crew of the *Donner* was going to have a Ship's Party. Whenever the crew bought anything from the ship's store, the money went into a fund that could be used for anything that would bene-fit the entire crew, like the records the mailman and I bought, or anything else for recreational purposes, like a Ship's Party.

A Ship's Party wasn't just a party; there would be dancing, beer, liquor, wine, and food. The crew could bring guests, and it would be quite a party. The party would also be a Ship's Fight. Some guys went to these things just to settle grudges; they used being drunk as an excuse. No master-at-arms went to these parties; they knew what was in store for them.

Bob, Jones, Pot, and a bunch of others—even Slim, who never went out of his way to be friendly—wanted me to come to the party. I told them that I wasn't going. I knew that we were in Virginia, which was segregated, and something told me that if I went to this party I was going to get into a fight. The steward's mates and stewards wouldn't be there; as I said before, they weren't considered part of the crew.

Instead of going to the party, I went on liberty in Norfolk and returned before the crew. When they got back, it was a mess. They were drunk and hollering; some had bloody noses, swollen lips, and black eyes; some guys in the lower bunks got urinated on. That was a pretty typical Ship's Party. Needless to say, I was glad I hadn't gone.

During the time that we were tied up at the pier in Norfolk, we had a Cold Iron Watch, which was standard procedure when a ship was tied up for a while. The ship was put on shore power, and all internal power sources were shut down. When the boilers went cold, the Cold Iron Watch officially started.

Engine room watch was set for 0400 hours. This meant that the engine room would start to get up steam at 4 A.M. It took only a few hours to get up steam enough to pop the safety valves. This was not always a good time for the engine room gang, for the crews of other ships would be watching the smoke come out of the smokestacks, and they could tell if you were getting up steam correctly; this was called the efficiency haze. If a mistake was made, you could hear a roar from the crews of the other ships. They could tell if you had made a mistake by the color of the smoke. If you didn't make a mistake, they would applaud when the safety valves popped.

The Navy had come up with a new title for motor machinists: enginemen. We helped the engine room personnel by standing watch and performing some of their functions. We recorded data like the pressure on various gauges, the temperature and salinity of the water outside, and temperatures in the engine room and in what was called the shaft alley. These readings were taken hourly. It was not hard work, but it was steady; it kept you busy.

Packard asked me one day, "How come you're a third-class petty officer? You should be a second- or first-class petty."

I said, "I don't know. I guess I never went for it."

He said he felt that I should be promoted, and he was going to put me in for second class.

Now, nobody is given a rating in the Navy; it is earned. And because of what you have to go through to get a rating, it can't easily be taken away. There was a standard procedure for promotion tests in the Navy between 1943 and 1948. Normally you would go to Personnel, and they would give you the manual for that rate and also a progress test; you studied the manual at your own pace and took progress tests as you went along. If you messed up on a progress test, you went back to the manual, studied some more, took that part of the test again, and so on until you were satisfied that you had passed. When you felt that you were ready, you went back to Personnel, and they would give you the actual test for the rating.

At least that's how it was normally done, and that's how I had always done it before. This time, though, they wanted to handle it a little differently. They gave me the manual for the second-class rating, but whenever I wanted to take a progress test, I had to get one of my division officers to go down to the engineers' office, and he would give me the test there. I had never done it that way; I had never heard of it being done that way; other guys on the ship were taking tests for all kinds of ratings at this time, and they weren't doing it that way. I went along with it for a while, studying five or six chapters and going down to the engineers' office for tests, but finally I said to hell with it—they can keep the rating; they don't want me to have it.

One day there was an announcement for all hands to fall in at quarters, which meant that anyone not on watch had to change into undress blue uniforms and form on the five-inch gun deck. When I went to change, I couldn't find the key to my locker. There were spare keys in the ship's office, though, so I ran up the ladder, heading there, and met the executive officer in the passageway. He said, "Boy, where are you going?"

I said, "I'm going to the ship's office to get my spare key so I can change uniforms and fall in on deck."

He stared at me. "Boy, you're going to be swimming around here. Now get below. I don't want to see you up in Officers' Country again."

"But sir, I won't be able to fall in on the deck unless I change into my undress blues."

"Boy, did you hear me?"

"Yes, sir." I turned around and went below to my compartment.

Packard came down after we got under way and asked why I hadn't been on deck. I told him that I had lost my key and that when I went to get my spare, the executive officer told me to get below. I didn't tell Packard the rest of what he had said.

This incident frightened me. It took about two weeks for me to get over it. For example, one of the things I was supposed to do was record the temperature on the bearings of the drive shaft or propeller shaft of the ship. We had two engine rooms; I was in the port-side engine room. To read the bearing temperatures, I had to go up the engine room ladder to the main deck, go aft, and then go down a ladder into the shaft alley. But after the incident with the executive officer, I wouldn't go into the shaft alley. I wouldn't go onto the deck at all after dark; I wouldn't even go up to the signal deck for the nightly movies. If it had been a crew member I would have ignored the threat, but it scared me, coming from an officer. I have the utmost respect for naval officers, but this officer had frightened me.

We sailed next to Charleston, South Carolina; we never knew the reason for the trip. When I went ashore on the liberty boat I saw a large throng of Negroes around the landing area; they were dressed in white. Something about them bothered me, but I never figured out what it was. I stood on the landing, looked around, and said to myself, *This is not the place for me.* I got back on the liberty boat and returned to the ship; I just had a feeling that I would get in trouble if I went ashore.

The next day we were under way for Jacksonville, Florida, also a one-day stop. I didn't get liberty while we were there, but I didn't mind. We weren't sure why we made this trip either, and before we knew it, we were back in Norfolk.

Then I developed a case of acute appendicitis. I immediately had surgery at the Portsmouth Naval Hospital, just across the bay from Norfolk. During my recovery the *Donner* left port. I didn't know where she had gone, nor did I know that my gear had been put in the hospital's storeroom per normal procedure. A few days later I was released from the hospital and given a Pullman ticket to Boston, where the *Donner* had gone. I was also given meal tickets and directions to the ship. I took a ferry to Cape Charles, Virginia, and boarded the train for Boston.

I had no trouble finding my ship; she looked good. But at first I couldn't find my gear, and I was afraid that I had been transferred. Then I found it in the hospital's storeroom. Nothing had changed after all. I even got my same bunk and locker.

Boston had a lot of old buildings, and as in all of these so-called free states, all of the Negroes lived in one section of the city. There was nothing exciting going on except the jazz show at one of the bars off Tremont Street. Red Allen and his group were playing. This was where I spent my time; since I had just gotten out of the hospital, I wasn't ready for any women.

We left Boston after a week; the *Donner* was to be put in dry dock in Portsmouth. Part of the preparation for putting a ship into dry dock is removing all ammunition. In these situations the Navy used an area just off Cape Henry, Virginia, for dumping ammunition. I was assigned to the unloading detail and got the opportunity to see the ship's magazine. The magazine was a large compartment; there were racks of ammunition throughout. A fine white powder covered everything. I noticed that everyone in the magazine except the first-class gunnery petty officer was Negro; all of the stewards and steward's mates were there, and me too. This confirmed what I had heard about the magazine being the general-quarters station for Negroes.

Since I had never been in this area before and didn't know any of the procedures, I watched the other guys to get an idea of what I was supposed to do. Some of them were releasing the locks that held the ammunition onto the racks when I noticed a couple of guys smoking. I said, "Hey, man, you can't smoke in here."

One of them said, "Aw, come on, Newt, it's all right."

I said, "Fuck you guys, I'm getting the hell out of here." I went up on deck and worked there. I was nervous until the ammunition had all been unloaded. Since it was night when we finished, we went into Hampton Roads and dropped anchor. The next day we went into dry dock in Portsmouth; our boats were stored in Little Creek.

When a ship goes into dry dock, the crew is moved into dorms on shore; shipyard workers do most of the work. The only time the crew returns to the ship is for special work, and for symbolic watch (guard duty), which is maintained the whole time. One reason for removing the crew is to allow the ship to be fumigated. The ship is sealed, and a gas is used to kill rodents and roaches; they are usually plentiful, especially near the galley.

While we were in dry dock, another Negro seaman was assigned to the ship. He was assigned to the deck force and worked under the first-class boatswain's mate who had given me so much trouble. I knew as soon as I heard he was on board that he was going to catch hell under that first-class boatswain's mate. The boatswain's mate had been waiting for someone to pick on, and Shorty, the new guy, was his man.

Shorty was assigned to all the shit details. Whenever there was a chipping hammer going, you would find Shorty at the end of it. He was assigned to boat duty and any work party that came up. This went on constantly, but Shorty could take it; the good part about it was that it didn't bother him. We became good friends, I guess because we were the only Negroes on the ship who weren't steward's mates. We hung out together quite a bit, on ship and ashore.

When the dry-dock work was completed, we took the ship out for a shake-down. This was a test run to see if everything was functioning properly, especially things we had worked on while the ship was in dry dock; shakedowns last a few days so that all systems can be thoroughly checked out.

We then returned to Norfolk and put the civilian workers ashore. We learned that we would be going next to Annapolis, Maryland, to pick up some midshipmen at the Naval Academy; we would be going on the midshipman cruise to the islands, with gun practice on the way. I told everybody that Annapolis was only about thirty miles from Baltimore; I could go home on a liberty.

The next morning we were off to Annapolis. Before dropping anchor we ran the "measured mile" opposite the Naval Academy; a distance of one nautical mile was marked off there for ships or boats to run in order to adjust various instruments and engine speeds. After the measured-mile runs, we had liberty. About ten of us Negroes got into cabs and went to Baltimore.

"OK, Newt, where are the women?" they asked me.

"I don't know," I answered.

"This is your hometown, and you're telling us that you don't know where to find girls?"

I said, "Not the kind of girls you guys are talking about. I never dealt with any of them here."

"Damn, Newt. Any other city in the world, you can find 'em as soon as we get ashore. You got any idea where to look?"

"We could try Pennsylvania Avenue; that's the main street for Negroes," I guessed.

We started at one end of Pennsylvania Avenue and went to the other with no success. I didn't know if it was because we stood out (we had on white uniforms), or because there were so many of us, or because there just were no prostitutes to be had. The guys felt that they had seen enough of Baltimore and wanted to return to Annapolis. I called my mother and told her we were returning to the ship. We got into cabs and returned to Annapolis.

The next day we picked up the midshipmen and set our course for Guantánamo Bay, Cuba. We were to meet the fleet on the way and hold fleet exercises. As part of these exercises, we had gunnery practice. Five-inch, fifty-caliber, forty-millimeter, and twenty-millimeter guns were all fired. The five-inch gun target was a huge float that could be either stationary or towed by a ship; the *Donner* didn't hit it at all. Drones (six- to eight-foot models of planes) flew past for the other guns to shoot at; we didn't hit any of them, either. The *Donner* was reprimanded by the admiral. I was glad that this was peacetime, for the gun crews on that ship couldn't have hit a bull in the ass with a ping-pong paddle.

Sometime after our return to Norfolk from the islands, the ship had a "Family Day." All crew members of the *Donner* would be permitted to bring their families, girlfriends, or friends on board and spend the day. They could have lunch and dinner with us. Some of the white crewmen were going to take their guests out on the ship's boats, so I asked the stewards and steward's mates if they would like to take their guests out on one of the boats too, if I could get one. They answered yes. I went up to the boat pool office and asked if I could take a boat out. They said, "Sure, go ahead!"

There were only a few Negro guests on board. We were gone a couple of hours. We went out past Portsmouth, then over to Newport News. The water was too shallow to get up to Hampton. We went past Old Point Comfort then back to the pier where the *Donner* was tied up.

A new crew member came aboard about then, a chief master-at-arms. At first glance, you got the impression that he couldn't be trusted; we soon found out this was true. Nobody liked him. Apparently someone had a conversation with him about me; he constantly watched me. For about a week, every time I turned around he would be watching me. I would be down in the well deck on my boat; I would look up, and he would be on the catwalk watching me. Anywhere I went, I would see him. I said to myself, *This guy is trying to get something on me.* I had found out a long time ago that it's not what you do that gets you in trouble in the Navy; it's what you get caught doing. I knew I had to be careful, because this guy was after me. If someone follows you around constantly, sooner or later he is going to get something on you.

One day I was down in the well deck and lit up a cigarette. All boat crews smoked in the well deck, even though we weren't supposed to. Before I could get the smoke out, this MA jumped from the catwalk onto my boat and asked for my name, rate, and serial number. I went to captain's mast, and the captain gave me a deck court-martial. I received a $50 fine; the MA had succeeded.

. . .

One day I was down in the steward's mates' compartment talking, and I asked them why they never had a Ship's Party. They said they didn't know; they just had never had one, that's all. I told them all they had to do was go to the disbursing officer and tell him that they wanted to have a Ship's Party, and he would give them the money; the white guys did it all the time. Mitch, a first-class officer's steward, went to the disbursing officer. Sure enough, he gave Mitch the money.

The day of the party Shorty and I went into Norfolk early to find some girls for the party. We went past the place where the party was to be held. I looked at the building. It had a sign outside naming it as some kind of hall; actually it was only a two-story frame house.

The party started at 7 P.M. It was on the second floor; we went up the steps. At the top of the steps was a small room with the food and drink, and to the right was a larger room, where there were tables and a jukebox. On each table were two fifths of liquor. There was a special table set up for the captain; he came in with the disbursing officer.

By ten o'clock the party was really jumping. Then something happened in the small room. There were only about thirty people in the whole place, and all the guys had women, so we hadn't thought there would be any problems. But the noise from the small room was getting louder; it sounded like a fight. The captain rushed out from the big room to where all the noise was coming from, and everyone else followed. When we got to the door, people in the small room were trying to get out while we were trying to get in, and another fight started. The captain and the disbursing officer and all the rest of us were swinging. It was the sort of situation where no one knows what's going on, so you just hit the first person coming your way. You don't know why; you just hit him, that's all.

The captain finally made his way into the room, and the fighting stopped. All of the girls had been running down the stairs screaming, and this brought the Shore Patrolmen, who came in hollering that they were going to lock everybody up. The captain said, "These are my men, and I will take full responsibility for them." Then he ordered all us to return to the ship.

Back on board the *Donner* I went around to different guys trying to find out what in the hell had happened. One guy said someone had been opening a can of beer. The opener slipped and cut another guy on the hand. The guy who got cut hit the guy with the beer, and the fight started. Somebody was even swinging on the captain, and you just don't do that; hitting the captain is bad business. Since the captain was swinging, I guess it was self-defense on all sides. I never did find out what happened to all the beer and whiskey we had in that place, and to be truthful, I really didn't care.

I was still trying to get in with some of the civilians in Norfolk. Whenever I went into Norfolk, I would go to the best bar on Church Street where the civilians went. I would sit there, looking and listening. One guy who came into this bar seemed to be liked by all the customers and the people who worked there. I decided that he was the key I needed to get away from those whores on Church Street. I started talking to him, and through him I started to get friendly with the barmaids, who wouldn't talk to me before. One evening someone mentioned the fact that the Ravens (a singing group) were going to be at an auditorium in Norfolk; they were talking about going to see them. I told them that I liked the Ravens too, and they invited me to go along. We all met at the bar the night of the event and went to the auditorium to see the Ravens and dance. I had my foot in the door.

One night in Norfolk I was walking a girl home, and I had to go to the head. We were in front of a food place. I told her to wait while I went in and used their head. I asked one of the guys working there where his restroom was. He said they didn't have one.

I said, "You mean to tell me that you are serving food, and you don't have a restroom?"

He said, "That's right!"

I said, "I'll be damned." I went outside and looked around for another place but didn't see one.

We passed a narrow alley, about four feet wide and very dark. I went up the alley to the point where I couldn't see my hand in front of my face, and I began to urinate. All of a sudden, lights came on. As the lights came closer, I could see two white policemen with flashlights.

One said to the other, "Do you see that?"

He answered, "Yes, I see it."

The first policeman said to me, "You're under arrest."

I asked, "For what?"

"For indecent exposure."

I knew that no one could see me up this alley; the policemen couldn't even see me until they turned on those flashlights. But I came out of the alley with a policeman on each arm. As I walked past the girl I said, "See you later, baby."

The policemen took me up Church Street to a larger alley. This one led to another alley that ran parallel to Church Street. We walked toward Brambleton Avenue, where the police station was.

One of the policemen said to me, "You're one of those smart niggers, aren't you?"

I said, "No, I'm not smart."

Then he hit me in the stomach with his night stick. I bent over, and the other one hit me across the back with his stick. When I straightened up, they did it again. I was looking at the lights on Brambleton Avenue, saying to myself, *Just let me make it to Brambleton Avenue.* These guys were really putting something on me in that alley. There was no one in the alley but the three of us. There wasn't even a dog back there.

I was glad when we got to Brambleton, and into the police station. They put me in a cell with some other guys. Directly across from us was a cell of women. I thought it was a damn shame to put men and women in cells that close together. We were only six or seven feet apart. All night long the guys and women were kidding each other. Every now and then one of the women would pull her dress up, and all the guys would holler. The guys right at the bars would shake their dicks at them. It was one hell of a night.

The next day we were taken downtown to the courthouse. When my case was called, I stood in front of the judge. When he called the two policemen, there was no answer.

The judge said, "Case dismissed. You can go."

I said, "Yes, sir," and turned around and started to the door. I wanted to run; I was hoping that those two policemen wouldn't come in before I could get out that door.

I got back to the ship, but I was late and had to go to captain's mast. The captain asked what had happened. I told him that these two policemen must have been waiting for some sailor to come up there, for they knew there was no head around there. I said that it was terrible how the police preyed on sailors over in Norfolk. They just locked up sailors for absolutely nothing.

The captain said, "Well, Newton, I guess I had better keep you on board ship for a while, because you seem to be getting into trouble over there in Norfolk."

I answered, "Sir, I can go to Portsmouth or Newport News. I don't have to go to Norfolk."

He said, "All right, I'm going to let you go this time. You can go now."

I said, "Yes, sir," and left.

That night I went back into Norfolk to find that girl. I never found her, so I caught the streetcar downtown to where I had to transfer. The transfer point was in front of a curb-service restaurant. You stood outside so you could watch for the streetcar while eating. I was the only one there at that time, and I ordered a coffee and a hamburger. I was eating when a policeman came and stood nearby. A streetcar pulled up and about seven sailors got off, raising hell. The policeman told them to quiet down. One of the sailors was a petty officer. He started to holler, "You heard what the man said; knock it off. He said to knock it off, so knock it off."

The policeman went to a nearby phone and made a call. I knew he was calling for the wagon, but that didn't bother me. I wasn't involved in this; in fact, I didn't know any of these guys.

The wagon came from the direction opposite the way I was facing. As I turned to look at it, I knocked over my coffee. I said, "Son of a bitch."

The policeman was standing next to me, and he grabbed me, saying, "There are some decent people around here."

I said, "If there are any decent people around here, I haven't met them."

I was the first one in the wagon. All that night I worried about what I was going to tell the captain this time.

The next day when we went to court the policeman told the judge that this one—pointing at me—said that if there were any decent people around Norfolk, he hadn't met them. The judge looked at me and said, "Ten days or ten dollars."

I had $9.50 in my pocket. I was taken back to the bull pen, where I tried unsuccessfully to borrow 50 cents. One guy told me he needed $2 to get out; if I loaned him $2, he would get out and come back and get me. I told him that wouldn't work. I asked if anyone wanted to buy my pea coat for 50 cents. Some guy gave me 50 cents, and I gave him a $20 coat.

I called the guard said, "Look here, Jack. I got my $10, let me out."

He said, "It costs $10.50. The 50 cents is court costs."

I went back to the guy who had brought the pea coat and told him he had to give me 50 cents more. He didn't argue about it, and I got out of jail.

I was late getting back to the ship again; I would have to go to captain's mast again.

The captain said, "Well, Newton, we're going to get under way soon. I'm restricting you to the ship till we get under way. That is all."

A sailor on the restricted list cannot go off the ship. He has to set up for the movies at night and clean up after them. He also gets assigned to any other detail that needs manpower.

The word going around the ship was that we were going to be taking some Marines to Newfoundland for winter maneuvers.

Now I got to see another procedure that I hadn't known about. We took off all the boats we used for the fleet and took them around to a naval base called Little Creek. Little Creek was where they kept the landing craft to be used in case of an emergency. There were no problems getting them started; they were all new VPs and LCMs. In just a few hours the ship was transformed from peacetime status to war status.

The Marines came up to Norfolk by bus. Three blasts on the ship's siren and one on the ship's horn, and we were on our way to Argentia, Newfoundland.

12 *Cruises*

Don't let anyone kid you about the winter weather in Newfoundland: it's colder than a whore's heart up there.

On our first day when we were ballasted down, we had a problem starting the engines on the boats. It was so cold that the engines would not light off, and we wore down the batteries in the boats. Until they were recharged we used jumper cables from the ship's power. No one involved in the planning of this operation had accounted for the subzero temperature and the effect it would have on the equipment. Picture, if you will, an invasion force that can't attack because their landing craft won't start. Somebody would have some explaining to do at the end of this exercise.

Meanwhile, we still had the problem of being unable to start the boats. All the engineers were called together to try to figure out a way to start them. We knew that if we continued to try to turn the engines over the way we were doing, we would burn the starters up. Someone suggested using ether to start the engines. I had never heard of this being done, but I did know a lot about ether; I knew it was highly explosive. The big question was who would be the one to go down into the engine rooms with a can of ether. He would have to hold the ether in front of the air intake of each engine. It was a job nobody wanted; even the ship's doctor was reluctant for anyone to try it, but Packard volunteered. To everyone's amazement, the ether worked.

We formed the boats in a circle, off from the ship, waiting to go alongside and take on Marines in rotation. It was colder out here than in the well deck of the ship. I don't think we could have put on any more clothing. We wore long underwear, shirts, dungaree pants, wool jerseys, and extra-heavy knee-length stockings. This was in addition to our fur-lined gear: boots, foul-weather pants, parka, elbow-length gloves, face mask, and hat. With all of this clothing, we were still cold. The one thing everyone feared was falling overboard; anyone who fell into this water would be in big trouble. It would be very hard to get you out, and you would probably freeze before anyone could get to you. I was concerned about falling overboard the whole time we were there.

This operation lasted only a couple of days. It was over as soon as the Marines had accomplished their objective: capturing and securing an airport. After the mission we had liberty in Argentia. There was nothing there but the airport. We went ashore, brought some trinkets, and returned to the ship. We then left for our next port: Halifax, Nova Scotia.

Halifax was very clean and quiet. There were a lot of fishing boats; it was a major commercial fishing port. We were in Halifax for two days to give the entire crew a chance to go ashore. I went ashore with about seven of the stewards and steward's mates. We didn't see any Negroes, so we stopped a cab and asked where the Negro district was, if there was one. The driver said that there was. We got into two cabs and were taken to the outskirts of Halifax. We ended up at some shanties unlike anything I had ever seen; they made all the shanties I had seen before look like mansions. These shanties were built more with hope than anything else. I had heard that there was no discrimination in Canada, but this burst that bubble.

Some of the people came out to greet us. When we asked about buying whiskey, we were told that we would have to go back into Halifax. We sent one guy back for four or five bottles. We spent a few hours going from house to house and then went back to Halifax. There was going to be a dance for the crew; this would be the first time that the entire crew had been at a dance together.

It turned out to be a very good affair, even though there were only about four Negro girls there. I met one of the girls; we danced, and I told her that we had to be back on the ship at 11 P.M. We went to her place; while she was undressing, I broke out laughing. When she asked what was so funny, I told her that I had never seen a woman wear long underwear before. She said that all the women there wore them. When you considered the weather in that place, it made all the sense in the world.

We returned to our home base in Norfolk, and I went into town on liberty. While drinking at Russell's, the bar where I had become a regular, some of the guys invited me to hang out with them that evening; they were going home with one of the barmaids for a few drinks. Her apartment was in Liberty Park. We were having a good time until one of the guys stood up and said, "I have to go in town and lock up a few sailors." I had always suspected that the Norfolk police played these games; now I knew it was true. The nerve of this black bastard making a statement like that! I hadn't known that he was a policeman, and I didn't care; I was ready to jump right on his ass. It took a few hours and quite a bit of whiskey to cool me off.

When everyone else started to leave, the barmaid asked how I was going to get back to my ship. I told her I had a weekend pass, and she said that I could spend the night. I forgot all about that cop.

After we had washed all the glasses and ashtrays, she went into the bedroom, and I went with her. As she undressed I was thinking, *Oh, boy, look at what I got.* But when we got into bed she said, "You turn over that way and go to sleep."

I said, "What?"

She said, "I'm not going to do anything, so you'd better go to sleep, or you can start walking into town."

I thought, *What a damn shame. Here I am in bed with a woman, and she tells me to go to sleep. I never heard of such a thing. She must be kidding.* I tried again, but she wasn't kidding. So I turned over and started thinking about that policeman. It was a damn shame the Navy let the Norfolk police do that sort of thing. The Navy could have stopped it. All they had to do was let the police know that if they continued this harassment of U.S. Navy personnel, the Navy would declare the city off limits. And I bet it would have stopped in two days. I finally went off to sleep. What a miserable night!

The next morning the barmaid made breakfast, and I asked her, "Are you sure you don't want to do anything?"

She said, "Yes, I'm sure."

We left for the bar, and I never got that close to her again.

Whenever we didn't have liberty, the main place to hang out was the tool crib. There were always a few guys sitting around, and there were interesting conversations. These things weren't planned; somebody would say something, somebody would have an answer, somebody else would have a thought about that guy's answer, and a couple of hours would pass so quickly that you didn't realize it.

One night the topic was the white man's intelligence. I said, "I think he's a dummy."

The guys started to grumble. "How you figure that, Newt?" one of them asked.

I didn't hesitate. "Take a Negro working as a porter in a factory. One night after everyone leaves, he pushes a certain button. This causes $50,000 worth of damage. When the white boss comes, the first thing the Negro does is put both hands in his hair and start scratching. He gives some stupid answer, and the more stupid the answer, the more the white man is going to believe him. That Negro knew that something was going to happen when he pushed that button, but the white man will never believe that a Negro is smart enough to push a button without being told."

They were quiet, so I continued. "Or take a case where a cop stops a Negro for speeding. When the cop comes up to the car he says, 'I smell liquor.' The Negro says, 'I do too, now that you have come up here.' The cop breaks out laughing and tells the Negro, 'Go on, but don't let me catch you speeding again.' This is a con act that the Negro has been pulling on the white man, so who's the dummy?"

Nobody could think of an answer.

Then the conversation turned to women, which is mostly what we talked about down in the tool crib. The conversation concerned a certain movie star whose picture was pinned on every locker door. The guys were saying what they would do with her or to her. One of the guys asked me if I would like to have her. I told them no because if I did, I wouldn't be able to tell anyone about her, and no one would believe me anyway; it would be the best-kept secret she ever had.

Somebody mentioned a party. "Hey, Newt, we're having a Ship's Party. Are you coming?"

Another guy said, "Yeah, Newt, you went to that steward's mates' party. How about coming to this party with us?"

"You should hang out with guys in your division," someone else yelled.

I said, "Well, I don't know."

They insisted. "Come on to the party; we want you to come. You haven't been to any of our parties." They gave me the address of the hall in Portsmouth where the party was going to be.

I decided to accept. "All right. I'll be there."

I told Shorty about the party; some of the white seamen had already mentioned it to him. He said that he wasn't sure whether or not he wanted to go. We talked about it, both unsure. After all, we were in Virginia, and these guys would be drunk; there could be some trouble, especially for Shorty and me. He kept saying that he would go if I would, and I kept wondering whether or not it would be worth it. The white guys were right: I had gone to the party that the Negroes had. If I didn't go this time, they would have a reason not to invite me to the next one. And I was the one who was always insisting that we should be included in activities; my words were catching up to me. On the other hand, if things got out of control, Shorty and I might not make it back to the ship.

We had a week to make up our minds.

The evening of the party Shorty and I went into Norfolk and got a bottle of liquor; we still hadn't decided whether to go or not. After we finished our bottle, I told Shorty that I was going. We caught the ferry to Portsmouth and found the hall easily. Two white girls were working in a check room just inside the door; they were shocked when we walked in, but after a minute they went ahead and checked our coats. Undisturbed, we walked into the main room, expecting someone to stop us. No one did. Once inside, I told Shorty that we should be with our divisions. When I headed over to where the engineers were, there were shouts: "Hey, Newt's here." I sat at the table with the guys I hung out with on the ship. They introduced me to their wives and girlfriends, and I had a very nice time. I probably would have enjoyed myself more if I had been more relaxed, but I kept expecting something to happen. I didn't see one incident, though.

When I got back to the ship I ran into Shorty, who had a lump under his eye. He said that he had gone into the head, and the captain had hit him, for no reason. I laughed and told him I would see him later. When I got to my compartment, I asked if anyone knew what had happened to Shorty. One guy said that when Shorty went into the head and saw the captain, he grabbed the captain's submariner's pin and said, "I want to talk to you"; that's when the captain unloaded on him. I had figured that Shorty hadn't given me all the details. I was still smiling when I went to sleep.

The next time I went to Russell's Bar, I joined the guys for drinks at another barmaid's house after closing. While we were there, a woman came in who knew everyone else there. After being introduced, we had a conversation, and I found out quite a bit about her. She was a college graduate, had a good job, and was married. When she was ready to leave, I asked if she could drop me off in town. She agreed, and we talked more in the car. This was the type of woman I had been looking for; all that time in Russell's had finally paid off. That night was the beginning of a wonderful time, even though it was brief. We had been together about ten times when she told me that she was uncomfortable with our relationship. It ended as quickly as it began.

We received word that we had to be in some maneuvers down in Puerto Rico, but first we were to proceed to Morehead City, North Carolina, to pick up some Marines. Again we were to take all of our boats to Little Creek and bring on board the wartime assault boats.

On the way down to Morehead City we had a payday, which meant there was a crap game. I always preferred shooting dice with the white guys. The Negroes liked to shoot on a blanket; a guy who knew what he was doing could shoot all day without making a mistake when he used a blanket. The white guys like to throw the dice against the bulkhead; there weren't too many guys who could set the dice that way. The white guys also would give better odds, like 2:1 or 3:2. I made more money shooting with the white sailors.

One day during this trip we were shooting dice in the bilge. The game had been going on a long time when the officer of the day walked up on us. He told everyone to freeze, so of course everyone took off like a bat out of hell, away from the officer. After I had run about fifty feet, I stopped. I thought, *It doesn't make sense for me to run. This area is brightly lit, and I'm the only Negro in the group. He might not recognize those other guys, but he sure as hell can find me.* The officer of the day kept running past me, chasing the other guys. I figured he'd put me on report and I'd have captain's mast the next day, but nothing ever happened. That was one of those incidents that I never could figure out; I was just glad that I didn't get in trouble. Whenever I think about that day, I start thinking that the white officers weren't all bad.

We were in Morehead City for a few days. The most memorable thing about the trip was that the one time I did have liberty, I went into town with some of the Negro sailors. They told me later that after a few drinks, I had wanted to fight everybody. I couldn't argue with them; I had blacked out, so I didn't remember anything about that night. They said that Mitch had had to knock me out to get me back to the ship.

We had one more thing to do before heading to the islands. The inland waterway comes out at Morehead City, and they wanted us to take our LCMs down the waterway from there to Camp Lejeune, pick up more Marines, and bring them back to Morehead City. The inland waterway was designed for small craft to travel from somewhere above New York to Florida without venturing out into the Atlantic Ocean. This portion of the waterway was only about fifty feet wide and wasn't very deep. We had to feel our way up the waterway, and we often ran aground. If we passed any civilian boats, we had to stop so as not to hit them with these fifty-ton LCMs. But we made it to Camp Lejeune, picked up the Marines, and returned to Morehead City, where the Marines boarded a troop transport. We did take some Marine officers on board the *Donner.*

Our next exercise was to be in Puerto Rico. There would be a stop at Saint Croix. Because the *Donner* was so slow, we left for Saint Croix while the rest of the fleet had gunnery drills at sea.

From the sea, Saint Croix is beautiful; the houses are painted in pastel colors, and the city seems to slope up from the sea. We anchored about a mile offshore, and I spent most of the day looking at Saint Croix. I was almost as fascinated as I had been watching the Parthenon. Maybe I was getting older; I was getting pretty good at standing on deck watching scenery.

While I was watching the people on the beach, an officer came on deck and stood next to me. Then a couple of other officers came along. A little later, they were joined by another. Pretty soon I was surrounded by officers. Without intending to, I overheard their conversation.

One young ensign asked the ensign on his left, "Did you hear that they're having a reception for us tonight?"

Before the second ensign could answer, the guy on his left said, "Yeah, it should be a pretty nice affair."

"The hell with that," the one in the middle said. "The Old Man said that the uniform is dress whites."

"Shit, I didn't know that," guy who had started the conversation said. "There's no way I'm going to put on my dress whites for a bunch of god-damned gooks."

"Count me out too, it ain't worth it," another said as they all left the railing and went below.

I had never been to the Virgin Islands before, so I wasn't exactly sure what they were talking about. I had a pretty good idea, though; the way they had said *gook* sounded a whole lot like *nigger*. I did know that the majority of the people on these islands were Negroes.

That evening, when the boat left to carry the officers ashore for the reception, they all went, and they had on dress whites. The captain must have laid down the law.

When I went on liberty that evening, I did the same thing I always did in a strange place: I headed for the back streets where the real people lived. I came upon some Virgin Islanders playing Calypso music with some unusual instruments. One guy had an exhaust pipe from a car or truck. Another had something that looked like a horse's jaw. One fellow had a jug-like thing; I'm not sure what it was, but I don't think it was really a jug. There were guys with drums, gourds, a trombone, a trumpet; one guy just had two sticks. They really sounded good!

Being a sucker for a parade, I followed them through the streets. We passed some stewards from the ship, who tagged along. We got thirsty following them and after a while took off in search of some of the rum that Saint Croix is noted for.

We found a nice little bar and started drinking. Pretty soon we met some girls who wanted to have some fun. They told us we would need a taxi, so we crammed into one cab and took off. The only place they could find to take us was a sugarcane field. It was pitch black; there was no moonlight. My white uniform stood out a lot more than the stewards' tan ones. As we split up, I was thinking that these girls could have found a better place than this.

My girl and I were into our act when someone yelled, "What's going on here?"

When I turned around to look over my shoulder, I was staring down the barrels of a shotgun. *Oh, shit,* I thought. I pointed to the girl and said, "We're not doing anything!"

The farmer lowered the gun, "Oh, I thought you were stealing my cane."

"No, we don't want your sugarcane; we're sailors," I told him.

"OK," he said, and left. By then I did need a drink of rum. We finished quickly, took the girls back to town, and went back to the ship.

While we were anchored off Saint Croix, someone got the idea of catching one of the sharks that constantly circled the ship. A chicken neck was put on a meat hook, which was then tied to a one-inch hawser line. This was lashed to the crane, and the hook was lowered into the water. A shark bit on it almost as soon as it was in. They hauled the shark up over the side, high enough for someone to slit his stomach open. His insides dropped out all at once. The inside of a shark is pure white. He was then lowered onto the deck. The captain, who had been watching the whole time, told us to get a fire axe and split the shark's jaws and to tie his tail down, because he could still be dangerous.

The axe bounced back the first few times they hit the shark's jaws. It took a while to split both sides of the jaws. Once the jaws were split, they pulled out the teeth and gave one to each of us standing around. I felt the shark's skin; it felt like coarse sandpaper. I kept the tooth, but as I watched the shark, for some reason I thought about the Japanese pilot who had torpedoed my ship during the war.

That evening my section had duty. I went to the board to see if I had an assignment. Sure as rain falls, I was assigned to Shore Patrol duty. I arrived on the quarterdeck to muster with the other Shore Patrolmen. The officer of the day approached me.

"Where are you going, Newton?" he asked.

I looked at him a while before answering. I was carrying a night stick and had on boots, a guard belt, and a Shore Patrol badge on my arm, and he was asking where I was going?

I said, "My section has duty, my name is on the Shore Patrol list, so here I am."

He said, "No, you have liberty tonight." He went over to his desk and took my liberty card from the file. He gave it to me, saying, "You have liberty tonight," with a tone of finality. I knew that I didn't have liberty that night, but I took the card and returned my gear to the armory. I got ready for liberty.

On the way into Saint Croix on the liberty boat, I was telling one of the stewards about what had just happened about the Shore Patrol duty. He said, "Newt, I've been sailing around these islands for about twenty years, and I have never seen a Negro Shore Patrolman on any of these islands. They don't want any Negro coming ashore showing authority. It would excite the local Negroes, and they don't want to excite them."

When we got to shore, I ran into the girl I had been with the night before. She told me that I wouldn't have to pay this time. I liked that but insisted that I wasn't going in that cane field again. She said that all we had to do was wait until dark, and we could go down to the beach. I wondered just how many good places she had to go on this island. We drank and talked. Later we went down to the beach until it was time for me to go.

When we got back to the ship, there was a guy in our compartment raising hell with all the white guys for having sex with black women. "You guys should be ashamed of yourselves," he said, "going over there and sticking your peters in those black girls." He told them that they should be ashamed to look a white woman in the face. I wondered who was looking at this guy's wife right now.

The next day we left Saint Croix and went about five miles to Charlotte Amalie, Saint Thomas.

I met one of the stewards in the passageway. He said, "Hey, Newt, how about going ashore with me after I get off?"

I said, "I'm going with some of the guys in my division."

"Keep hanging with those white guys, and you're going to get yourself in a lot of trouble."

I walked on, thinking that I was in a pickle about this. The Negroes thought that I should hang out with them, but the way I saw it, I was on the ship for the purpose of integration. Hanging out with the stewards was not going to get that done; association was the key. At least that was how I saw the situation.

I went ashore with several of the white boys in my division. We stopped in a bar, and I got into a conversation with one of the civilians. He asked me how could he get into the Navy.

"Just go down to the Navy recruiting station and sign up," I told him.

"I already did that; they wouldn't let me in," was his answer.

"I don't see why not. They let in a lot of Filipinos that can't even speak English."

"I tried and I tried, but they still won't let me in." He sounded desperate.

"Don't give up; keep trying." I left the table, feeling sorry for this guy. I thought *I* had had to go through a lot to get into the Navy.

We left that bar and went to another one. After a couple of drinks someone suggested going to Bluebeard's Castle. This place was really a castle; it sat on the side of a hill overlooking the town of Charlotte Amalie. There was a spectacular view of the town and the harbor. I realized that I was the only Negro in the club, and I knew that if I hadn't been with these white boys, I would not have been there.

The bartender was mixing a drink called a Zombie. He said that if you drink one, you get the second one free, but he advised against coming back for the second one. Naturally we had to hang around for the second one. The floor was crowded with people dancing. The popular song down there was "Mary Ann," a Calypso song. Everyone was doing the Calypso; they had me out there dancing with those white girls.

We left and went into town to a bar called the Paper Doll. Twenty or thirty guys from the ship were there; the *Donner* was the only ship in the harbor. We were buying drinks and having a nice time when the chief of my division came in with a girl, and they went to the middle of the bar. We were at the end of the bar. I went over to the chief and the girl and asked the chief if they would have a drink on me.

The girl said, "Get away from me. I don't fool around with niggers."

"What did you say?" I asked.

"You heard me. Get away from me. I don't fool with any niggers."

I slapped her, and to my surprise she went over three or four tables. I was so mad that I just blew up. "I'm sick and tired of this shit! Every time we go out to drink, you all come on with some shit, and I am tired of it."

One of the guys came up to me. "Newt, the girl's gone to get the police. They're gonna whip your ass. You better get out of here!"

"They're not going to whip me, they're going to have to kill me. I'm not going anywhere," I yelled. "Every time I come out I have to put up with that shit."

Another guy took me by the arm, "Come on, Newt, let's go back to the ship."

"I'm not going anywhere. You guys just leave me alone, and get the hell away from me."

The Shore Patrol officer came in. "Newt, you'd better go back to the ship before you get yourself into a lot of trouble."

"I'm not going back to the ship; just leave me alone."

The Shore Patrol officer, who happened to be the fleet wrestling champion, grabbed me, threw me over his shoulder, and carried me out of the bar. He put me in the jeep and took me back to the ship. When we got there, he told the officer of the day at quarterdeck to put me on report.

Now I really got upset. I remembered that the captain had told me that I could come to his stateroom anytime I wanted to, without asking anyone's permission, so I went straight to the captain's quarters. The captain opened the door and offered me a cigarette. That was the last thing I remember about that night.

The next day the word came over the PA system for me to muster on the five-inch gun deck for captain's mast. This was no surprise; I was expecting it. When I got before the captain, he was boiling mad about something—I had no idea what.

He said, "Newton, for your actions last night I should give you a general court-martial. That's too much trouble, so I'll let you go with a summary. You have a summary court-martial. That is all."

I said, "Yes, sir," and walked out.

On my way back to my locker I ran into the division warrant officer. He said, "Newton, I want you to know that we officers are not going to forget what you said in the captain's quarters last night."

Not only did I not know what had been said in the captain's quarters; I didn't know how they had overheard it. All of the officers seemed to be mad at me. *The next time a captain tells me to come to his stateroom,* I said to myself, *I won't even bother.*

I learned later that the girl who had been with the chief in the bar came down to the ship with the police. She tried to have me turned over to them, but the captain refused.

We left Saint Thomas and proceeded to Vieques Island, Puerto Rico, where we were to hold maneuvers. From the sea, Vieques appears unpopulated.

There were very high swells (waves) breaking on the beach, which could have been trouble for the landing craft. We would have to be careful not to get broached (turned sideways) on the beach. That wasn't our main concern, though; we were more worried about falling overboard. There were man-eating fish called barracudas in the water.

We loaded the troops, took them to the beach, then backed off the beach, running parallel to it, watching the action. I noticed that the Negro troops were handling supplies on the beach and the white troops were going forward. It was the same old story; these Negroes were supposed to be Marines, but all they did was handle the supplies.

Shortly after this a PL (personal landing craft) came up beside our boat. The guy on the PL told me that I was wanted back at the ship. The engineer came aboard, and I returned to the ship. When I got there the officer of the day told me that I was a prisoner at large, and that I was not to leave the ship under any circumstances. I watched the rest of the maneuvers from the deck.

After a few days we left for Kingston, Jamaica. I couldn't go ashore in Kingston, so I watched everybody else go. I noticed that the guys were coming back to the ship and quickly leaving again. I asked what was going on. Somebody told me that the girls didn't want money, they wanted onions. Before that night was over, every onion in the spud locker was gone.

After a few days we headed for Guantánamo Bay, Cuba. On the way to Cuba I was called up to the executive officer's office. I was told that a Marine lieutenant had been assigned as my defense lawyer, and that the court-martial would be held at Guantánamo Bay. I had a feeling that I knew how the court-martial was going to turn out. There wasn't a lot happening in my favor; the officers on the ship had made it clear that they didn't like what I had said to the captain.

The Navy didn't spare any expense for my court-martial. They brought in just about everyone who had been in the bar that night, but since the incident had occurred away from everyone but the chief, the girl, and me, there wasn't much those guys could say. One said that he had heard the slap, and some others said that the first they knew of the situation was when they saw the girl going over the tables. When the chief was asked about what had happened, he said that he hadn't heard anything; all he knew was that I had hit the girl. I just looked at him; it was impossible for him not to have heard what that girl said. When they questioned me, I told them just what had happened.

The court-martial was over quickly.

I went below and was changing when the guys who had testified came by to talk. They said that they hadn't wanted to go up there but had been ordered to do so. I thought it was real nice of them to come by and apologize.

Later the ship's yeoman came up to me and said that they had recommended me for a bad-conduct discharge. He wasn't supposed to be telling me this; if any of the officers knew that he had been talking to me, he would have been in trouble. The recommendation of the court-martial board had to go to fleet headquarters to be approved. It then had to go to the U.S. Navy Office in Washington, D.C., for final approval.

About a month later I was called up to the executive officer's office. He read me the penalties that the court-martial had recommended. I was to be demoted to an apprentice seaman (the lowest pay rate), forfeit all pay (I hadn't been paid since the incident), and receive a bad-conduct discharge from the U.S. Navy. He finished, and I left. I didn't react when he told me this, because I had known it, thanks to the yeoman.

After the court-martial, I had a lot of time to think. I remembered something that one of the white boys had told me when I came aboard. He said that even if I was right, I was going to be wrong. I thought back over the almost five years I had served in the Navy and realized that I still didn't know what freedom was. One thing I was sure of was that since the time I had first been assigned to the *Donner*, my relations with the white sailors had improved greatly. I also knew that association was the key, and that if Negroes were given the same training as the whites got, they could be just as good if not better. I certainly knew that I was better than good in my rating. But that was in the past; I couldn't do anything about it now. All I had to look forward to was the verdict from Washington.

I promised myself that I would not go home with a bad-conduct discharge. I didn't know where I would go, but it wouldn't be back to Baltimore.

While I waited, there were some changes on board. Another Negro fireman was assigned to the *Donner*, an electrician's mate striker, and my friend Shorty was transferred. That was good for Shorty, because that first-class boatswain had been giving Shorty trouble every chance he got. The new Negro fireman, Phillips, was assigned to the Engineering Division. He took the bunk next to mine. I could see that Phillips wouldn't have the same problems I'd had. He seemed to be pretty smart, and I thought he could hold his own. We became good friends.

I think it was a couple of months before I was again called up to the executive officer's office. As I walked into the office I was thinking, *Goodbye, Navy.*

The exec said that he had just received the result of my court-martial back from Washington.

I was thinking, *Oh, Lord, here I go.*

The exec said that Washington had reversed all penalties and had placed me on six months' probation.

I was grinning from ear to ear.

The exec spoke first. "Newton, under the rules of court-martial, you're entitled to a ten-day leave. Do you want it?"

"Yes, I do, sir. Thank you."

"Well, go get your gear packed. Go find the disbursing officer. Tell him that I requested that he bring your pay up to date. By that time I should have your leave papers ready, and you'll be able to leave the ship immediately."

I went to my locker; on the way I was telling everyone about my probation. By the time I got to my locker there was a crowd around me. I told them that I was going on leave and would see them in ten days. I was really excited.

When I told the disbursing officer what the exec had said, he paid me in five-dollar bills. I'm sure he had some twenties, but he just wanted to pull his ass with me. Sailors don't have pockets large enough to put that many five-dollar bills in, so I shoved them into my bag and got my leave papers and left the ship.

I reasoned that someone in Washington had realized that if a Negro was in a bar with twenty to thirty white sailors and he slapped a white girl in front of them and none of them protested, then something must have happened. I was thinking that everything the admiral had said at Great Lakes had come true, and more.

I went over to the naval air base to catch a plane going up to Washington. I couldn't catch a hop there, so I went over to the civilian airline and purchased a ticket to Washington. Having all my money in this bag was not working out, so I got a small paper bag from a clerk at one of the counters at the airport. Now I had all my money, about four months' pay, in a paper bag.

I don't know what I had been thinking about when I decided to fly to Washington. I had never flown before, and when that plane started to move, I would have given someone a thousand dollars to let me off. After a while I settled down, though, and began to like it. When the plane landed in Washington, I decided to fly to New York, so I brought another ticket. The plane I had taken from Norfolk to Washington was small, but the one I was taking to New York was large. It was one of the newer planes, a triple-tailed Constellation.

I stayed in New York two or three days with my brother, then went to Baltimore for the rest of my leave. When I got back to the ship, I got the word that we were going to make the midshipman cruise to Europe. Now we had to get our boats ready for the cruise, which was coming up in June.

13 *Midshipman Cruise*

Every summer the class of midshipmen who were about to become seniors took a cruise; this year's destination was Europe. We spent most of our time doing maintenance on the boats in preparation for the cruise.

One night during a storm a launch bringing some sailors back from liberty in Norfolk swamped. The boats from our ship were detailed to search for bodies, but because of the weather we couldn't search the day after the storm. It was still very cloudy, and we had to wait another day for the sun to come out and heat the water. As the water got warmer, bodies began to surface. A few of the sailors on the liberty boat had managed to swim to shore, but most of them had drowned. We recovered about thirty bodies. This was not a pleasant detail, and it reminded me of the war.

The midshipmen came by bus from Annapolis the day before we were supposed to get under way. I was told to report to the engineering officer. When

I got to the office, he told me that there was a Negro midshipman on the aircraft carrier *Philippine Sea* and asked if I would escort him into Norfolk. I readily agreed, since I was scheduled for duty that night. I was told to meet the midshipman, named Leroy Brown, at the foot of the gangway of the *Philippine Sea*.

When Midshipman Brown came down, I introduced myself. "My name's Newton, and I'll be showing you around. There are some things you need to know about Norfolk. This is Virginia, you know, and we have to ride in the back of the bus, and—"

"I'm well aware of what goes on here," he interrupted.

I tried to explain. "I just wanted to make sure. Negroes are only allowed in certain areas of the city; you need to know this stuff before we get there."

"Thank you. As I said, I'm aware of how things are here."

"OK, let's go." I just hoped that he really did know what he was doing. I knew only too well how much trouble Norfolk could give a Negro.

Brown spotted a pinball machine in a drugstore while we were walking up Church Street. He wanted to play the machine, so we went in. We played for a while, taking turns on the machine. I soon got thirsty.

"Do you want to get a drink?" I asked as I finished a game.

"Not now. I'll get a soda later. Thanks." he said.

I scratched my head for a minute. "I'll be right back," I told him.

"OK."

I went a few doors down to a liquor store and got a pint. When I got back to the drugstore Brown was in the same spot, still playing that machine. When no one was looking I would take a sip from my bottle and then tuck it back into my pants.

"Say, Brown. You know we're getting under way in the morning. Do you want to go find some girls?"

"No, I don't want a girl."

This was starting to irritate me. I had to stay with this guy, but he didn't drink, and now he didn't even want a girl the night before we were to leave. It looked like all he wanted to do was play that machine.

"I tell you what. You stay here and shoot pinball; I'm going to find a girl. I won't be long, though."

"OK."

I left and found my steady girl. When I returned to the drugstore, Brown was still in front of the pinball machine. I waited around watching him play until he was finally ready to return to the ship. Brown and I may have both been Negroes, but we definitely had different ideas of how to have fun. He wasn't the type of guy I could hang out with for long; he didn't say much and didn't want to do much.

The next morning the rest of the fleet went somewhere for gunnery practice while we headed for Lisbon, Portugal.

Lisbon was interesting. There were steps everywhere; Lisbon had a lot of small hills, and the sidewalks were steps. As you walked around, you were always going up and down steps, and it seemed as if everyone was passing out cards advertising the houses of the different madams. In the houses, the girls gave out pictures of themselves. I had never seen that before.

We were in Lisbon for only two or three days. For the first time in my life, I saw women work as hard as men at physical labor. The women in Lisbon unloaded ships, and they brought the cargo off on their heads. American women wouldn't even think of doing that kind of work. We tried to make dates to meet some of these women after they got off work, but I don't think any of the guys kept the dates.

Our next destination was Villefranche, on the French Riviera. We arrived in Villefranche about 9 P.M. and dropped off about ten or twelve boats, including mine; then the *Donner* continued to Nice without us. Villefranche was another one of those places where the water was only about a foot below the landing area. That wasn't surprising, because it was on the Mediterranean, so there was no tide. I remember thinking that if they ever got a bad storm with high winds, the area around the waterfront would really be in trouble.

There were about twenty-five or thirty of us who had been dropped off from the *Donner.* We didn't have anywhere to sleep, and it was approaching midnight. We went into a bar, which was about to close. I caught the eye of one of the waitresses as she was leaving, so at least I had company. Less than forty-five minutes after setting foot on French soil, I was lying in a grassy spot with a French girl, looking out at the Mediterranean. In the morning I realized that we were in a park. She went her way, and I went back to the boat to await the arrival of the fleet. It was a sight to see the fleet come into position and drop anchor.

For this exercise I had orders to report to the battleship *Missouri;* for the four days that we were in Villefranche, I was a part of the *Missouri's* crew. We took our boat out to the *Missouri* and reported to the officer on the quarterdeck, who got on the PA system and called someone. A lieutenant came down and told us that the four sailors with him would take responsibility for the boat. He said that we had liberty while the *Missouri* was in Villefranche.

One of the sailors took us below to find bunks. After taking a shower and changing, I told my coxswain that I was going to look the ship over. It took me ten minutes to get lost and about an hour to find my way back to the main deck. I hadn't realized how large a battleship was. The *Missouri* was huge; there were a few thousand men in the crew.

We got duty the second day, even though we were supposed to have liberty the whole time we were there. Our orders had been changed: we would be ferrying sailors and midshipmen between the *Missouri* and shore until 1500 every day.

That night I ran into Midshipman Brown at an outdoor café with a group of other midshipmen. I spoke to him briefly, then went on my way. I also ran into one of the steward's mates from the *Donner*. He was with a beautiful French girl. He asked how I liked her, and I had to be honest: she was the best I had ever seen. Later I ran into Jones, one of the white guys in my division. We went into Nice together. We met a couple of girls and ended up in a hotel. As I was coming out of my room, Jones was coming out of his; we exchanged girls and went back for more.

After returning to Villefranche, we went into a club that had a live band. I was kidding around with the band members and found myself sitting behind the drums. I thought I could play, but as soon as the music started, the band and I found out better. They stopped playing, and I left the bandstand.

Later, while I was standing around, a woman called me over to her table. She was with a good-looking woman. She told me that this was her daughter and asked if I would like to marry her. I was thinking yes, I would, but I could just imagine life with a white wife in Baltimore; I knew that wouldn't work. One of the guys from my ship came by. I whispered for him to call me outside. In a few minutes he came up and said that Bob wanted to see me outside. That was my chance to get outside and back to the ship.

The next night I went ashore and saw the same steward's mate who had been with the good-looking French girl. His head was bandaged. He said some sailors from one of the ships had jumped him because he was with a white girl. They didn't harm the girl.

Later I was drinking at a sidewalk café with a girl I had met. She was telling me that the French hate Americans because of their attitude; they think they own the world.

"Americans are so arrogant; I hate them," she said.

"I'm an American, so that means you hate me."

"No, you're different."

"What makes me different from them? I'm an American, too.

"You are not like the white Americans; I can't stand for them to touch me. No French people like the Americans, but they spend money, and we need the money. If it were not for the money, we would not have them here."

"I guess you're right," I said. The tone of the conversation had changed; we had a few more drinks and went to a hotel.

Afterward I walked down a small street and saw Midshipman Brown in a café. I joined him; we were the only two Negroes in the place. A chief petty officer came in with a group of sailors. While talking to them, he called out to someone to bring his "nigger-loving ass" over there. Nobody in the café said anything; everyone just looked. I looked at Brown; his expression never changed. The drunken chief was still hollering, "Hey, bring your nigger-loving ass over here." Finally someone went over to talk to the chief, who left the café. I told Brown I would see him later, and I left.

The next time I was ashore I rented a paddleboat. They were popular; lots of people were out in them. While I was out, a yacht came by, and I saw a colored girl aboard. I didn't pay her any attention. I had seen a lot of colored girls in the area. Most of them had their hair like a bush; somebody told me that they were Moroccan, from North Africa. By that time I was pretty far from shore and tired of paddling. I decided that I didn't like the paddleboat. I promised myself that I would never get on one of these things again, if I ever got this one back.

When I got back, I met some of the stewards from the *Donner*. One of them asked, "Hey, man, did you see Josephine Baker while you were out?"

"Who is Josephine Baker? I've never heard of her," I answered.

"There she is, on that ketch out there." One of the stewards pointed.

I looked. He was pointing to the ketch that had passed me when I was out. I saw her but still didn't know who she was.

It was our last night in France, and I had to find my last French girl. It didn't take long. The Riviera was like Miami: there were women everywhere. I found one and went back to the *Missouri*.

The next day the *Donner* was to get under way. I got hung up on the *Missouri* because the disbursing officer had not taken the currency exchange money back to the French bank. (You were supposed to exchange your American money for French money while you were on the ship, but no one did that. You could get more foreign currency on shore than on the ship.) We took the disbursing officer ashore and waited for him while he went to the bank. We were tied up to the waterfront. There was a huge crowd to see the fleet pull out. I was sitting on the cockpit behind the coxswain, next to the flag. I rode there because I could see all the gauges relating to the engines. After the disbursing officer returned, we shoved off for the *Missouri*. The coxswain had to show off for the crowd; he walked the boat away from the dock. As the boat turned, the flag wrapped around me. I had seen the flags of many countries, but this was the best one to be wrapped in. The crowd was waving and hollering as we headed for the *Missouri*.

We dropped off the officers and guards on the *Missouri* and headed for the *Donner*. She was under way at slow speed; we caught up with her and pulled into the well deck. They pulled up the tailgate and began to ballast up.

When everyone was settled down, the PA system crackled. "This is the captain. I have just received word from the admiral. He says that because we did such a fine job with the boats he is giving us a four-day leave in England. We are heading for Plymouth, England. That is all."

When we left Norfolk, there had been midshipmen and Navy reservists on board. The midshipmen had been transferred to other ships while we were on the Riviera, but the reservists were still with us. There was a Negro reservist in the group. From the beginning he had said that he had to get to London; he had a girlfriend there, and he had to take her something. It was a money belt full of money. He took the reserve trips every year trying to get to England, and this time he finally made it. He was lucky to be going to England; it wasn't on our schedule.

I went ashore in Plymouth with this reservist and some other guys, just to look around. The Germans had torn Plymouth up; they had really put something on Plymouth. The most remarkable thing about the place was that even though it had been destroyed, it was *clean*. It was spotless; even the vacant lots were clean. There was no trash anywhere. It was amazing how American cities could be so dirty and this city here, with all this destruction, could be so clean.

While walking around, we met a couple of British girls. They had on black dresses with black stockings, which turned me off. In fact, all the people we saw we were dressed in black. England had lost two-thirds of her manpower and was in a severe depression. I gave one of the girls some money and told her goodbye.

The Negro reservist suggested going to London. We all agreed and boarded a train for London. When we got to London, all these girls rushed up to us and said, "We've been waiting for you." I was thinking that this was a lie because they hadn't known we were coming to London. Suddenly I remembered that I had heard the same thing when I got to Washington, D.C., and I realized that there were simply no men around. So we all had girls.

We went to the Paramount Dance Hall. I could see right off the bat that I was going to have a problem: I couldn't understand what my girl was saying. I'd had no problem with the French girls. They spoke English very well, but here in England I couldn't understand the people.

We brought some liquor and went into the dance hall. I guess it was around seven or eight o'clock in the evening when we got there. We danced until around twelve, when the dance hall closed. We came out, got into these things called hackneys, and went across Charing Cross to another dance hall and danced till four in the morning. The bands playing in those dance halls were very good; I was thinking that the American bands had better watch out.

We still didn't have any rooms, so we got back into the hackneys, and went back across Charing Cross, where we found a hotel. Around eight that morning, we went out for breakfast. The girl with me ordered beef curry. I tried it, too. It was very spicy, but it wasn't bad.

The reservist's girlfriend finally showed up. I was surprised to find out that she was colored. "You came three thousand miles to see a colored girl?" I asked in disbelief.

He just smiled; he was so happy to see her that nothing anybody said could bother him. They went off to the side to talk. I knew that she was going to be happy once she started to count all the money in that money belt; there were thousands of dollars.

I couldn't believe it when the girl with me said we were going back to the dance hall; it was ten o'clock in the morning! But we went back and danced until teatime. We had to stop then; everything in England stops for tea. Once while we were on a train the train stopped at teatime. The engineer and the crew went somewhere and got tea and crumpets (a type of cookie).

Later the girl took me on a walking tour of London. She was a bundle of energy if I ever saw one. We walked all over London and talked about a little bit of everything. We ended up in Hyde Park, where she showed me a statue of President Roosevelt. I told her that there wasn't a statue of him in America yet. I looked at that statue and thought, *Yeah, you're gone, and I'm still in all this mess.*

We had beef curry again and went back to the dance hall.

"I'm going up to Glasgow," the girl said. "Come with me."

"I can't do that."

"I'll take care of you; my father owns a pub."

I said, "Girl, I can't go to Glasgow with you. What would I look like, deserting the Navy and running around in Glasgow? I would look like a cherry in a bowl of milk."

She said, "I have money, I'll take care of you—"

"No." I interrupted. "First of all, they would have no trouble finding me. The second thing is that I could never marry a white girl anyway. The first time you called me out of my name, I would nail you to the wall."

"I would never do anything like that," she protested, but I didn't want to hear it.

I answered, "Yeah, that's what you say now." The incident with the white girl in the Virgin Islands was still fresh in my mind; I wasn't taking any more chances.

The next day's routine was the same: Eat beef curry for breakfast, go to the dance hall. Have beef curry for lunch, go back to the dance hall. Have tea, dance. Have beef curry for dinner, then go back to the dance hall. This girl was a freak for beef curry and dancing.

The following day was my last, so we didn't go to the dance hall. I was glad; my feet had blisters from all the dancing.

We took the subway to the train station. I had been on subways in America, but they were nothing compared to these English subways; over there in England, you went down about ten thousand steps to get to the trains.

When we got to the station, we learned that we had about two hours before our train left for Plymouth. We went outside to wait. There was a group of about sixteen of us standing around with nothing to do. Someone got the bright idea that if we stood close together, two us could get in the middle and have sex standing up without anyone knowing. We tried it, and it worked, so each of us had sex right there, just outside the train station.

After four memorable days in London, we headed back home. Our course was set for Norfolk, Virginia.

Two days out of Plymouth we ran into a terrible storm. This storm created more problems than normal because someone had forgotten to move the plate that covered the drain in the well deck. The well deck was the large area where the boats were kept. There was a drain in the bottom of the well deck to let water out. Whenever the ship was in port, the drain was covered with a steel plate measuring about five feet by three feet, and an inch thick. The purpose of the plate was to keep debris from clogging the drain. But now, since the plate was still covering the drain, the well deck was being flooded. Waves were breaking over the fantail every two minutes, and they estimated that we were taking on fifteen hundred gallons of water with each one.

No one was aware that the plate was on the drain until the word came over the PA system for all hands to muster aft for a bucket brigade. I couldn't believe my ears; with all the pumps on this ship, they were calling for a bucket brigade? We put on our life jackets and went aft.

The ship was all lit up with floodlights. As soon as we got aft, everyone could see what had happened. The portable P500 pumps were scattered all over the deck. They were all over the deck because the deck crew had gotten frustrated and thrown them aside. I had found out long ago that these pumps were no good. You couldn't get them to start; they were a waste of the Navy's money. The other, permanent, pumps that were normally used to remove water from the well deck wouldn't be of any use to us either as long as the plate was covering the drain.

There was about three feet of water in the well deck, enough to float the boats. The last boat in, which happened to be mine, was tossing about; the line securing it had snapped. Someone tried putting five-inch hawser lines on the boat, but they just snapped like string. Remember, this boat was an LCM. It weighed a few tons. It was causing quite a bit of damage as it bounced around.

We in the bucket brigade were bailing as fast as we could, and the deck crew was still trying to start the P500 pumps, but we weren't making much progress. I looked up to see the captain watching me; if he thought I was going down there on that boat, he was sadly mistaken. My boat was a total wreck, and it had damaged the three boats in front of it.

From the ship's light all you could see on the water was gray foam. Sailors say that when the water is foaming, that's a sign of a terrible storm. I had been in some bad storms before, but none like this. The Atlantic is supposed to have the worst storms in the world. The old saying is "The Pacific is terrific, and the Atlantic is all it's cracked up to be." North Atlantic storms are the worst of all, and we just happened to be in the North Atlantic.

Our efforts were worthless, because we were taking on water a lot faster than we could get it out. Someone got the idea that if the cable on the crane was long enough, we could hook it onto the LCM and pull it up against the other boats. That would keep it from bouncing around, and then someone could go down and put a hook on the drain plate. Whatever we did would have to be done quickly, because the other boats were starting to float.

The deck crew played out the cable from the crane; it was long enough to hook onto the LCM. They were able to pull the LCM up against the other boats. One of the guys jumped in and hooked the drain plate onto the cable from its crane (the deck plate had its own crane). Once the plate was hooked, the crane lifted it off easily. Everyone yelled and screamed; this little adventure was over. I wondered why the well deck was designed the way it was. Why would someone make it like that? It could have sunk the ship. I promised myself that if I ever got my feet on dry land again, I'd stay there.

When we got back to Norfolk, I was called up to the executive officer's office. I couldn't think of any reason why I should have to go there.

"Newton, the fleet is going. Your enlistment is up in August, and we won't be back in time for you to be discharged. If you're going to reenlist, there's no problem; you can go. If you're not planning to reenlist, you'll be sent to the outgoing unit until your enlistment is up. I need to know what your plans are."

"Sir, I'm not going to reenlist," I told him.

"Very good. That is all."

I saluted, he saluted, and I left the office. There was no way I was going to reenlist for four more years of this shit.

Two days later I was told to pack my things; I had been transferred to the naval receiving station at Norfolk. As I left the ship there was a group of guys on deck saying goodbye. Phillips, the Negro fireman who had come on board not too long before, was there; I looked at him and thought, *You'll have to take the ball now. It's a hell of a lot better than when I came aboard about two years ago, but I just can't take any more.*

I put my bags in the jeep and went to the receiving station.

14 *End of Service*

I checked in at the naval receiving station and found that in Norfolk, the Navy hadn't changed much. White sailors still slept in one barracks and Negroes in another. I made up my mind to just settle down. I was going to be here until sometime in September, when my probation from the court-martial ended; then I'd be discharged. It was July when I reported, so I had a couple of months to lie around and try to stay out of trouble.

There is absolutely nothing to do in a receiving station. At the Norfolk station, roll call was at eight o'clock every morning, and liberty started at four in the afternoon. I was given a detail to clean the barracks every morning. Sometimes I was the only one on the detail; there was no one else there.

The Navy hadn't stopped trying to get me to reenlist; I had to go and watch "Shipping Over" movies. They showed waves breaking over the bows of big ships at sea. The movies were nice to watch, but they had no effect on me. They didn't show the discrimination behind the bulkheads.

Receiving stations are the same all over the world: fellows come and go. A group came in on their way to Balboa, Panama, and the first thing they did was call me Old Man. I started to think that maybe they were right. I was twenty-three years old, and my hair was turning gray; I guess I was an old man. Every day someone in this group would try to get me to reenlist and go to Panama with them. The guy would say, "Come on and go down to Panama with us and have a good time."

I would say, "I think we could have a nice time in Panama, but I'm not going. I've had it, and I'm getting the hell out of here while I have the chance."

One of the guys played the saxophone. He tried to teach me how to blow a sax. He had some sheet music and everything. According to him, the easiest song to play on a saxophone was "Tea for Two." The notes were CAB, CAB, BGA, BGA, CAB, CAB, GE. I tried my damnedest to learn that song, but I played so badly that he told me to practice in the head.

One day a request came for ten people to serve at a funeral for a Negro sailor who had died. Six pallbearers and four riflemen were needed. I had never served as a pallbearer; neither had anyone else in the barracks. One of the officers got a manual and read the procedures to us. He showed us this slow step that we would be using while carrying the casket. Within an hour we were put on a bus, and each man was given a pair of white cotton gloves.

We made the journey to the church with no problems. Once we arrived at the church, though, we noticed that it had very steep steps. As we attempted to carry the casket up the steps, it started to slide back; it was difficult to hold with the cotton gloves. All the people around were murmuring, but we made it in and decided not to wear the gloves when we took the casket out. It seemed as if the whole world was watching as we took the casket out, but we made it easily because we had removed the gloves. We put them on again when we reached the graveyard. The riflemen fired several shots over the grave in a salute, and we returned to the base.

The probation was starting to worry me. It was only a matter of days before I was to be discharged, and I wanted to go into Norfolk. I was getting tried of staying on the base. I knew, though, that I could get into trouble in Norfolk without doing anything. The one thing I didn't need now was trouble. Well, I was determined to go into Norfolk, and I knew just what I was going to do: find a woman and come right back to the base. I went into Norfolk and found the girl I was looking for, and we went to a room. After we finished, I had a couple of beers and went back to the base.

During my time on the base I had a lot of time to think things over. As I reviewed the five-plus years that I had spent in the Navy, I reached the conclusion that I hadn't done too badly. I had done what they had asked at Great Lakes and at the naval service school in Hampton. I had tried to be "better than good," and I had tried to use my head in making decisions. Like any other man, I had made mistakes, but looking at my military career as a whole, I think I did what the Navy wanted.

Time after time I had been put in situations where I was the only Negro among the white sailors. I never tried to please them; I just did my job. I had never thought that I would have any close white friends, but I did, and I did miss them. I'd had to take many insults—most of them intentional, some accidental; they all hurt. I didn't appreciate being called a "good nigger," but I had learned that many whites had been raised to think of me that way; integration was a big adjustment for them, too.

I had experienced many things in the Navy that should be changed. For example, the manner in which courts-martial were conducted really needed to be changed. The accused sailor should have the benefit of a trained, competent, and impartial lawyer, especially when the potential penalty involved prison time or a discharge. One badly conducted court-martial could wipe out all of the years that a man had spent serving the country and could prevent him from getting a decent civilian job after being discharged.

Discrimination in the Navy should be totally abolished as quickly as possible. The practice of using Negroes as steward's mates and cooks was particularly degrading. Men should be allowed to learn any skills for which they show aptitude, and then should be allowed to work in those areas.

One of the biggest lessons I learned from my Navy career was that it is no fun being the first to do anything, especially when it comes to social change.

During those last days at the receiving station, something surprising occurred. An aviation machinist's mate striker came through. This guy had been a master sergeant in the Air Force before he switched services and joined the Navy.

The Navy wouldn't give him a petty officer's rate, and this angered him. As I said before, the Navy does not give you a rating; you earn it.

What made this significant was that I already knew this guy. He was the first person to teach me about tools and engines. When I was about twelve years old, he used to work on cars and motorcycles in the alley behind his house in Baltimore. Now he was in the Navy without a rating. After all the time he had spent in the military, I outranked him; this didn't make any sense to me. He borrowed some money from me to go on liberty, and I never saw him again. He went AOL (absent over liberty).

There has always been a controversy about which service was integrated first, the Army or the Navy. I've always thought that it was a matter of perspective; it all depends on what you consider *integration* to mean. President Roosevelt let Negroes into the Army Air Force as pilots before he let Negroes into the Seaman-Fireman Branch of the Navy. On the surface, then, it would seem that the Army was the first to integrate. But one must remember that the Negro pilots only flew in all-Negro units. Even though the Navy took longer to let Negroes into technical areas, the few Negro sailors in these areas (including myself) served side by side with their white counterparts.

The discharge process started three days before my enlistment was over. This consisted of a series of physical examinations and more reenlistment movies. I got a scare during one of my first exams. While I was having my eyes checked, the pharmacist's mate said, "We're going to hold you."

"Why?" I asked, about to get upset.

"Your eyesight is bad; it has changed since you came in."

"Look, man, just put down that my eyes are OK, and let me get out of here."

He gave me a strange look; I don't know what he put on that paper, but I passed the eye test.

By that time I had seen so many movies of ships at sea that I probably had them memorized. The photography was great and the scenery was beautiful and the whole thing was in color, but I knew the story that wasn't shown on the film; I knew what went on below decks. I knew about it, I had had my fill of it, and there was no way on God's green earth that I was going to reenlist.

Although I believed that association was the key to integration, I didn't think that I would ever live in an all-white neighborhood or attend an all-white school. I am never comfortable unless there are other Negroes around. I was comfortable in Norfolk, much as I hated the place, because I was around other Negroes there. And I was always comfortable at home in Baltimore; sometimes I could go for days without being around white people there. But as I've said before, I was never comfortable during the time that I was assigned to the *Donner.* Discrimination was happening twenty-four hours a day aboard that ship. I felt that people were planning things against me even when I was asleep. The only times I felt relaxed aboard the *Donner* were when I was around the steward's mates. Whenever there was a disturbance on board, I would go down and sleep in their compartment. I felt safer there; I just couldn't trust the white guys after they had been drinking. Maybe I was being too cautious. But I wasn't about to take any chances. I was not ashamed of this; to me it was just common sense. If I hadn't learned anything else, I always remembered Wickline's warning: "You can't beat them all."

I don't know for a fact that any Negroes were killed during the integration of the Navy, but I have a feeling that some were, and that the incidents are buried in the Navy's files. Some of these men are probably listed as having been killed in the line of duty, whether the deaths actually occurred in combat or not. During the period that I served on active duty, other Negroes were sprinkled throughout the Navy, and I'm sure they weren't all as lucky as I was. There were many occasions on which I could have been killed and no one would have known the difference, so I'm sure that luck was involved.

On 24 September 1948, at approximately 10 A.M., I walked out the gate of the naval receiving station in Norfolk. Once outside the gate, I turned and saluted. I saluted because I loved the Navy; I loved it the whole time I was in, and I still love it.

I don't know where this thing is going or how it is going to get there or who is going to take it, but one thing is for sure: it will have to be better than good.

15 *Reflections*

When I returned to Baltimore, I found that not much had changed. Everyone in my family had jobs. I lay around for a while, then enrolled in a GI school for house painting. I had almost finished the school when my father got a job as an apartment-house superintendent in New York City. I went with him.

My father stayed in New York City for only a year. When he returned to Baltimore, I remained in New York as the apartment-house super. I stayed until June 1951, when I got a job as a diesel mechanic's helper at the Coast Guard yard in Baltimore.

I got married in January 1953 and went to work for General Motors in March of that year. I worked for GM for thirty-nine years. During that time I became the first Negro to be a supervisor at a GM plant in the South.

From my marriage, I have five children: three daughters and two sons. One of my sons is a lieutenant commander in the U.S. Navy. He is now second in command of ships larger than the ones on which I served.

During my time in the Navy, it was rare to see a Negro officer; now there are Negro officers of flag rank. I often think of the many speeches we listened to in which we were told that we had to outdo the white sailors, no matter what. Many times we were told that our actions would determine the opportunities that other Negroes would be given. When I think about those speeches and some of the hardships we had to endure, I remind myself that I helped to lay the foundation for the accomplishments of today's African-American sailors.

ABOUT THE AUTHORS

Adolph Newton served in the U.S. Navy from 1943 to 1948. After his military service, he worked for General Motors in Baltimore for thirty-nine years, becoming the company's first black foreman south of the Mason-Dixon line.

Winston Eldridge, a native of Richmond, Virginia, served in the U.S. Army as a mortar crewman from 1976 to 1980. Now a resident of Mt. Rainier, Maryland, he is the author of an autobiographical story published in the anthology *Children of the Dream: Growing Up Black in America.*